Henry Collins Walsh

The last cruise of the Miranda

A record of Arctic adventure

Henry Collins Walsh

The last cruise of the Miranda
A record of Arctic adventure

ISBN/EAN: 9783337108038

Printed in Europe, USA, Canada, Australia, Japan

Cover: Foto ©Andreas Hilbeck / pixelio.de

More available books at **www.hansebooks.com**

NUMBER

OF THE FIRST HUNDRED COPIES OF THE

FIRST EDITION.

COLLISION WITH THE ICEBERG.

FROM A DRAWING BY G. W. PICKNELL.

The Last Cruise

OF THE MIRANDA

A RECORD OF ARCTIC ADVENTURE

BY

HENRY COLLINS WALSH

WITH CONTRIBUTIONS FROM

Prof. Wm. H. Brewer, of Yale; Prof. G. Frederick Wright, of Oberlin; James D. Dewell, Hon. George W. Gardner, Prof. B. C. Jillson, Dr. F. A. Cook, Capt. Geo. W. Dixon, Rudolf Kersting, Dr. R. O. Stebbins, Maynard Ladd, Arthur R. Thompson, Russell W. Porter, Carlyle Garrison, L. J. W. Joyner, Samuel Orth, and Chas. B. Carpenter.

Profusely Illustrated from Photographs taken on the Trip.

MDCCCXCVI
THE TRANSATLANTIC PUBLISHING COMPANY
NEW YORK
63 Fifth Avenue
LONDON
26 Henrietta Street, Covent Garden

COPYRIGHT 1895
BY
JAMES D. DEWELL.

CONTENTS.

	PAGE
THE LAST CRUISE OF THE MIRANDA. HENRY COLLINS WALSH	9
CAPTAIN DIXON'S LOG	135
ATMOSPHERIC DUST IN THE ARCTIC REGIONS. Professor William H. Brewer	148
GLACIAL OBSERVATIONS IN LABRADOR AND SOUTHERN GREENLAND. Professor G. Frederick Wright	162
THE GREENLANDERS. Frederick A. Cook, M.D.	172
A GREENLAND CEMETERY. James D. Dewell	180
THE ESKIMOS' TEETH, AND OTHER NOTES. R. O. Stebbins, D.D.S.	186
THE FLORA OF SOUTH GREENLAND. Samuel P. Orth	190
NOTE ON THE INSECTS OF SUKKERTOPPEN. L. J. W. Joyner	194
THE FINDING OF THE RIGEL. Russell W. Porter	196
THE TRIP TO HOLSTEINBORG. Maynard Ladd	203
ICEBERGS. Arthur R. Thompson	208
A GREENLAND SUNDAY. Charles Blake Carpenter	210
OUR ADVENTURES AT SUKKERTOPPEN. Carlyle Garrison	215
THE ILLUSTRATIONS. Rudolf Kersting	218
A LETTER FROM HON. GEORGE W. GARDNER	222
A LETTER FROM PROFESSOR B. C. JILLSON	225
THE ARCTIC CLUB	229

DEDICATED
TO
COMRADES ON THE MIRANDA AND THE RIGEL.

THE LAST CRUISE OF THE MIRANDA.

CHAPTER I.

It is a comparatively easy matter to organize an Arctic expedition in the city of New York, but it is quite another thing to get the expedition well into the Arctic regions and bring it safely home again. This requires a happy combination of circumstances, which the uninitiated are not apt to take into consideration. There was probably not an individual who had joined "Dr. Cook's Arctic Expedition of 1894" who for a moment doubted that the expedition would really be in Melville Bay on the scheduled time, and a connection with Lieutenant Peary and his party was looked upon as a matter of course. But, as Robbie Burns aptly puts it:

> "The best laid schemes o' mice and men
> Gang aft agley."

Quite a number of mice, as well, indeed, as their larger cousins the rats, had laid their plans to accompany the expedition; though to the credit of some, be it said, that with wise forethought they deserted the ship on the very day of sailing, and thus brought fear and dire forebodings to the hearts of superstitious sailors. But who then, except these wise rats, dreamed that a single solitary iceberg among the almost countless numbers that would be passed on the way would wilfully crash into the *Miranda*, and so delay matters by the damage inflicted as to force the expedition to give up its cherished plan of piercing into really far northern latitudes ; or again, who among the human beings dreamed that the ship would ultimately come to grief upon some sunken rocks off the bleak coast of Greenland, and thus end the expedition in disaster?

THE MIRANDA.

But this, as Mr. Kipling says, is another story, or rather one to be told later on.

At the start it may be well to state briefly the objects of the expedition, which, though they were not accomplished, except in part, still made up a very attractive prospectus. The main objects were : To study the Greenland glacier system, the inland ice-cap, the glaciers and icebergs ; to map out and explore a part of the unknown coast of Melville Bay, and to photograph, sketch, and study the Eskimos, and the animal and vegetable life to be found in the northern regions.

The Peary camp was to be visited, and the latest news concerning that expedition was to be brought back to the United

States in advance of the Peary party. A search was to be undertaken for the young Swedish explorers, Björling and Kallestenius, who had boldly skoaled to the northward in a crazy kind of a tub, and passed into the great Arctic silences, never to be heard of again. During this search a part of the unknown coast of Ellesmere Land was to be explored. Then the great game to be found in the Arctic regions, such as polar bear, walrus, reindeer, seal, caribou, etc., attracted quite a number of sportsmen to the expedition, among them such wellknown hunters as Professor L. L.

DR. FREDERICK A. COOK.

Dyche, of the Kansas State University, whose Western hunting experiences are related in "Camp Fires of a Naturalist;" E. A. McIlhenny, and Robert D. Perry.

The officers of the expedition were: Dr. Frederick A. Cook, commander and organizer of the expedition; Professor William H. Brewer, of Yale; Professor G. Frederick Wright, of Oberlin College, and Professor B. C. Jillson, of Pittsburg, geologists; Professor L. L. Dyche, Kansas State University, zoölogist; E. A. McIlhenny, of Louisiana, ornithologist;

Samuel P. Orth and B. F. Staunton, of Oberlin, botanists; Professor Elias P. Lyon, of Harvard School, Chicago, biologist; Dr. Jules F. Vallé, of St. Louis, and Dr. R. M. Cramer, of New York, surgeons; Professor L. J. Joyner, of Poughkeepsie, entomologist; Russell W. Porter, of Boston, and Robert DeP. Tytus, of New Haven, surveyors; H. C. Walsh, of New York, historian. Rudolf Kersting, of New York, was the official photographer, and Charles K. Reed, of Worcester, Mass., and J. A. Travis, of New York, were the taxidermists.

Other members of the expedition were James D. Dewell, of New Haven; Hon. George W. Gardner, ex-Mayor of Cleveland, Ohio; Ashley C. Clover, ex-Prosecuting Attorney of St. Louis; G. W. W. Dove and A. A. Freeman, of Andover, Mass.; Willis A. Reeve, of Patchogue, L. I.; William Bryce, Jr., of New York; Maynard Ladd, John R. Fordyce, H. D. Cleveland. Frederick P. Gay, of Harvard College; C. P. Lineaweaver, T. J. Lineaweaver, A. B. Brown, H. W. Dunning, Philip Evans, C. J. Rumrill, A. P. Rogers, A. R. Thompson, of Yale College; R. D. Perry, of Phillipston, Mass.; S. G. Tenney, of Williamstown, Mass.; Chas. B. Carpenter, of New York; Professor Charles E. Hite, University of Pennsylvania; G. M. Coates, G. H. Perkins, Howard Bucknell, of Philadelphia; R. O. Stebbins, of New York; W. H. H. Armstrong, of Newburg-on-Hudson; William J. Littell, of Washington, D. C.; Benjamin Hoppin and A. A. Sutherland, of Baddeck, C. B.; J. A. Travis, Jr., of New York; Walter S. Root, of Cleveland; F. B. Wright, of Oberlin; Carlyle Garrison, of Merchantville, N. J.

Carl Garrison, the last mentioned, was by far the youngest member of the expedition—a boy of but thirteen years of age. As his parents are old friends of mine, he went along under my care, and I had every reason to be proud of my young charge. Through all our various trials, dangers, and rough experiences he showed a courage and discretion far beyond his years, and accepted all manner of hardships with cheerfulness and with calm philosophy. He was dubbed the "Mascot." Who the more powerful spirit of evil in the shape of a Jonah was, has not yet been finally determined.

Perhaps the real Jonah was the *Miranda* herself, if a Jonah can be of the feminine gender. Certainly the name itself is suggestive of hidden reefs and tempests, and the vessel's previous history had been decidedly unfortunate. She was built for the Red Cross Line, in Liverpool, England, in 1884, and had hardly been put into service between New York, Halifax, and St. Johns when she ran on rocks off Point Judith. Later she struck on rocks in Hell Gate and sank,

CAPTAIN WILLIAM J. FARRELL.

but was raised at considerable cost. She collided with an iron steamer, and later with a schooner, and it was she who towed Leary's raft from Nova Scotia in 1887. The raft pulled the fastenings out of the *Miranda*, went to pieces, and became a serious disturber of traffic. She lost her good name and passenger trade after these accidents, and was finally rented out as a frieght steamer, running between New York, Jamaica, and Central America. Is it any wonder that, with such a singular penchant for rocks and collisions, she should finally have come to grief upon a sunken reef off the coast of Greenland? The captain of the *Miranda* was William J. Farrell, and the first officer, George Manuel.

OUR ESKIMO FRIENDS

The expedition started from Pier 6, North River, New York, on the afternoon of July 7. This was several days later than had been expected, but the *Miranda* had been tardy in a voyage from Central America. Of course, quite a crowd of people had collected about the pier, friends and relatives of the passengers, and a number of others were there out of curiosity to have a look at the vessel and its occupants.

A party of four Eskimos, consisting of a father and his two daughters and a youth, who were being taken back to their homes after assisting in the spectacular effects of a lecture tour, came in for a great share of attention, and submitted patiently to unceasing cross-examinations, for they had learned to speak English fluently, perhaps to their regret.

At length the signal was given for all to go on shore who were not going with the expedition, and the pause that came before the actual start gave a stout man on the wharf an opportunity to let off a few mild jokes at our expense. He persisted in looking upon the expedition from a humorous standpoint, and was aided and abetted in his point of view by a Fourth of July jag which had not yet entirely deserted him. "What in the name of Hades do you want to go to the North Pole for anyway," he shouted, "when ice is only two dollars a ton in New York?" Little did he know how dearly ice would cost us off the coast of Labrador later on. But when the start was actually made, and the *Miranda*, instead of backing out, as was intended, headed directly for the dock, hitting against two or three smaller craft on her way, his delight knew no bounds. "Are you going to hunt polar bear in Wall Street?" he shouted in high glee. Something unlooked for had happened. The signal wires going into the engineer's room, which had just been renewed, had been unaccountably crossed, and the engineer had thus received the reverse signal from the one intended. However, after threatening to entirely demolish some smaller craft, and after a great deal of bellowing and shouting, and not a little swearing, matters were rectified, and the *Miranda* backed out, swung, and started on her career, amid cheers and wavings and confused shoutings of farewell from the shore.

We steamed through Long Island Sound, and outside of Nantucket. The usual course is through Vineyard Sound, but an accident to our compass caused the captain to change the course.

The first days out were not crowded with incident, as is but natural on the ocean. The air was so balmy and the water so smooth that there was but little seasickness, though here and there men were stretched on steamer-chairs looking with jaundiced eyes upon the wrinkled sea. Most of the huntsmen, with a restless energy, kept up for several days a continual rifle practice, and shot at any shining mark that offered. Our deck, bristling with polished gun-barrels, resembled that of a pirate ship.

HENRY COLLINS WALSH

On July 9 several whales appeared and broke the monotony of the watery expanse. Many of them rose so close to the ship as to become targets for the sharpshooters, and a chorus of volleys saluted their advent, seemingly to the satisfaction of both parties concerned; for the whales spouted and dipped in answer to the salutes accorded them, and seemed not a whit the worse for the broadsides poured into them. In the afternoon a large swordfish almost ran into us, and also went on his way rejoicing, after receiving a baptism of fire.

The next day, Sunday, broke clear, calm, and beautiful, with hardly a ripple on the surface of the sea. The day passed without an important event, except that a small and select band of stokers and firemen seized the occasion to break into the wine-room, where they remained to scoff while others prayed, with the result that a free fight was indulged in, shortly after which one of the firemen disappeared. All sorts of rumors spread regarding the missing man, and it was generally believed that he had jumped overboard as a result of a drunken frenzy. He was several days afterwards discovered hiding in the hold, and deserted the ship promptly on our arrival at Sydney.

The next morning we were off the coast of Nova Scotia, and it was cold, foggy, and dismal. Our whistle was kept constantly blowing, and many soundings were taken. The gloom of the fog seemed to hang even over the breakfast-table until it was lifted by the genial Professor Brewer, of Yale. The Professor was the autocrat of the breakfast-table, and many a word of wit and wisdom fell with unconscious ease from his lips;—one of those rare men upon whom learning sits easily and gracefully, without weighing down in the least upon a delicate and keen sense of humor. To him we were indebted for much useful information upon all manner of subjects, as well as many a hearty laugh. On this occasion the laughter was raised unconsciously: but the story is too good to be left untold. The Professor sat at the head of the table holding an egg up to the light and eyeing it curiously. "See," he said to a professor next to him, "the wonderful provision of Nature in mending eggs," and he dilated at some length upon this provision, and passed the egg to let his brother professor inspect the shell, beneath an aperture of which another shell had apparently formed. "I have had a varied experience with hard-boiled eggs," said the Professor's brother in arms, "but this is certainly the hardest egg that I have ever seen," and he hit the egg a crack with his knife,

GROUP OF PROFESSORS.

but the knife rebounded. Professor Brewer then took the egg in hand again, and struck it a resounding thump with a heavy plated spoon. "Why, by Jolly," he exclaimed, "it's a china egg!" And then the inextinguishable laughter of the gods arose; but notwithstanding, the Professor finished his lecture upon Nature's method of mending eggs. It is needless to say

NORTH SYDNEY—CAPE BRETON ISLAND.

that in spite of the vigorous thumps it had received the particular egg in question needed no mending. Had it ever been hatched, a Shanghai rooster, perhaps, would have been the natural result.

"How well this crowd seems to get along," remarked a man opposite me at table, "in spite of the fact that before leaving New York scarcely one man in the crowd knew another."

"Well," said an Englishman upon my right, with the slow deliberation of his race and the air of a man who had given the subject careful consideration—"well, but we are a very superior crowd, you know." There was no dissent from this opinion.

Late in the afternoon of July 11, we steamed into the beautiful harbor of Sydney, one of the finest harbors in the world. A ray of the light that never was on land or sea seemed to have broken from the unknown void to shed its glory on land and sea and sky. On either hand the dual town of Sydney stood bathed in the dying light, and out in the harbor, suddenly, as if by magic, a gleaming French man-o'-war loomed into sight, "clothed in white samite, mystic, wonderful."

It was evening when we ran alongside of a wharf at North Sydney; for we had to take in a supply of coal here, as well as live stock and provisions. A speedy outpouring there was, as everybody was delighted to get a chance to stretch his legs, and North Sydney was quickly overrun by what looked like a band of pirates, for every one rushed on shore in sea-clothes. It did not take the crowd long to discover a restaurant, and soon there gathered here a festive throng who managed to sing and eat at the same time; next to the dining-room was a sitting-room furnished with a melodeon, which was kept in constant service by some musical members of the company. Suddenly there passed by the windows a band of the Salvation Army, and then there was a general rush. Grave professors, students, and sportsmen all joined in a grand triumphal march in the wake of the Salvationists, and lifted up their voices in a hymn to the tune of "Marching through Georgia." It was an extraordinary procession as it passed along the main street chanting to the accompaniment of a most vigorous and well-meaning, if erratic, band. Never before, perhaps, had this section of the Army of the Lord gathered in so many stray sheep.

I shall never forget the look of joy upon the face of an old salt who marched at the head of the procession beating a bass-drum with a nervous energy, as if he were thumping the very devil himself. At length a little, low meeting-house was reached, and when we had filed in and taken our seats the usual singing and clapping was gone through with. Pale, nervous-looking women, clad in the ungainly uniform of the Salvationists, with a wild, fanatical look in their eyes, hopped up and down on the stage, clapping their hands and chanting. Then came an address from the captain of the band, a strange hotch-potch, interspersed with many "glories" and "amens." He pictured the glories of the hereafter for the faithful soldiers of the Lord, and the eyes of the pale women gleamed with the light of hope and anticipation. "If there is joy in heaven," said the captain, raising his voice, "over one sinner doing repentance, what must be the joy in heaven when a soldier of the Salvation Army enters into the pearly gates? I can picture myself after death ascending upward, and a voice saying to me, 'Who comes here?' and when I answer, 'Jim Watson is coming,' oh, I can hear the echoes ringing through heaven—'Jim Watson is coming, Jim Watson is coming!' Oh, I tell you, friends, there will be exceeding joy in heaven upon that day!" And so he went on in his simple egotism. Indeed, I hope that Mr. Jim Watson's reception in heaven will be more enthusiastic than the one he was accorded by his hearers; for the natives of Sydney did not appear to respond heartily to the enthusiasm of the Salvationists. In fact, the people of Sydney seem to have made up their minds about this life and the next one, and perhaps they prefer to solve both of these problems by the lights that have already been given them.

There was another subject upon which the inhabitants of Sydney seemed to have made up their minds, and that was that we were a band of rash and foolhardy men, doomed to certain destruction. An iron ship, they declared, was not fit to make the voyage to the Arctic regions; it would be smashed by the ice. We smiled at such prophecies then, but later on we took them more seriously. One ancient oracle, a prophet of wind and wave and ice, who appeared to have honor even in his own country, was appealed to for his opinion. After the manner of many another oracle, he shook his head, gave a significant look, and said solemnly that he did not like to express his opinion in our presence. Had he doomed us to certain death he could not have thrown a deeper gloom upon the assembled company.

From North Sydney to Sydney proper is a pleasant half-hour's ride by ferry. At Sydney is a fine summer hotel, which had just been completed at the time of our visit. It is run by a Bostonian, Colonel Brownell Granger. Indeed, Boston capital seems to be doing a good deal for the development of Cape Breton. A party of four of us drove out to some rich copper-mines in the vicinity—a fine drive through a rolling and beautiful country—and were taken about the mines by the manager, Mr. Isaac P. Gragg, also from Boston. The mines are operated by a Boston firm, the Eastern Development Company. We were allowed to inspect them thoroughly, and descended the shaft, in the bucket the miners go down in, to the depth of six hundred feet. It was, of course, as black as pitch soon after we left the mouth of the shaft; but we each held a candle in one hand, and held on to the chain of the bucket with the other. We were rigged out in oilskin suits before descending, in order to preserve our clothes from contact with the slimy sides of the tunnels, and resembled a religious procession as we slowly walked on a narrow rail along the winding slippery tunnels, holding the lighted tapers before us. When we had been carefully hoisted to the welcome daylight again, and after we had removed our oilskins and washed the oozy copper slime from our hands, we adjourned to the country residence of the genial host of the Sydney Hotel, who was giving a lunch that day to a party of mining engineers and the lady members of their families. We had a delightful lunch, and were most agreeably and hospitably entertained. As we were seated on the broad veranda enjoying some of Colonel Granger's choice cigars, a Scotch bagpiper chanced along, with a company of two young men, an elderly woman, and a very venerable and silver-haired dame. It was a veritable pied piper who had appeared among us, and he soon had his little company dancing a unique and vigorous Scotch breakdown. The very old dame in particular danced with remarkable vigor, and displayed unlooked-for agility and friskiness.

> "And the gray grand-sire skilled in gestic lore
> Hath skipped beneath the burden of four score."

It was wonderful to behold this venerable girl skipping with graceful agility beneath her burden of four score. I am somewhat her junior, but I should not have liked to have engaged to dance her down. She was apparently as fresh after the dance as at the beginning of it, though she must have tramped a good distance that day, for we were many miles from town. We took a picture of the scene; but this, together with by far the greater number of photographs that were taken on the expedition, is with the *Miranda* at the bottom of the sea.

Sydney is a very attractive place, with green sloping banks that run down to meet the still waters of a beautiful cove—waters so deep that the largest vessels can anchor within a few yards of the shore; and here British and French warships are to be seen during the summer. Now that the town possesses a commodious hotel, furnished with every modern convenience, it must become a popular resort for sportsmen and tourists. There are plenty of salmon and trout in the adjacent streams, as well as fine salt-water fishing; then, as regards hunting, there are partridge, snipe, woodcock, curlew, and plover to be found in abundance, while within a day's journey are the magnificent hunting-grounds of the North Cape. Here is an immense tract covered with primeval woods, where bear, moose, and caribou wander about at will. The interior of these forests has never been fully explored, and but rarely echoes to the crack of the huntsman's rifle.

The people of Cape Breton Island are mainly of Scotch descent, and mining and fishing are their chief industries. The island is completely seamed with veins of coal, and the enormous mines at North Sydney run far out under the sea. These mines are also owned by an American syndicate. About a mile from North Sydney live a tribe of Mic-Mac Indians, who support themselves by making baskets and other utensils and trinkets. They are entirely independent, and are fairly intelligent. The chiefs and sages of the tribe dwell in little houses, and the others content themselves with wigwams.

We took in a supply of coal, some provisions, and live stock, at North Sydney, and then went gayly on our way, feeling that we had sufficient resources to take us up to the North Pole and back again if need be. It had been the original intention to go from Sydney through the straits of Belle Isle; but so much ice was reported that Captain Farrell made his course around Newfoundland instead. On the morning of Sunday, July 15, the forbidding and frowning coast of

MATE MANUEL AND PILOT DUMPHY

Newfoundland loomed up before us through a fog. As one of our compasses needed repairing it was decided to run into the capital city, St. Johns, in order to have the necessary adjustments made. The city is snugly hidden in a beautiful harbor behind high hills, and is a sudden revelation after entering the narrow channel that flows into the harbor. At the mouth of this channel we beheld our first iceberg—a very small affair when compared with the countless numbers that appeared to us later; but as it was the first one, and as we had not then formed standards of comparison, the baby berg created much excitement, if not enthusiasm.

We remained at St. Johns long enough for the party to land and stretch their legs for a few hours. The city presents a fine appearance from the harbor, but it has not yet recovered from the terrible fire which swept it in 1892, and whose devastations are only too apparent when a landing has been effected. A great many ruins are to be seen, especially of public buildings which were swept away; temporary and unsightly small wooden structures have been erected until better ones come in course of time; for St. Johns has not risen out of its ashes with the rapidity of Chicago and Boston; the mills of God grind slowly there, and the rapidity of Yankee methods is unknown.

At St. Johns, though we were there but a few hours, we were greeted again with all sorts of dire prophecies concerning our folly in venturing northward in an iron ship. It was, therefore, a considerable relief to all on board when Dr. Cook returned from a pilgrimage to the shore, bringing with him a veteran ice-pilot in the person of Mr. Patrick Dumphy, who had been mate of the *Kite* on Peary's first expedition in search of the Pole, and who was looked upon as a standard authority on Arctic navigation. Mr. Dumphy's services had been secured as ice-pilot, and he proved to be an oracle, something upon the pattern of the famous Jack Bunsby, guide, philosopher, and friend to our old friend Captain Cuttle. Mr. Dumphy's oracular manner, and the significant nods that accompanied his Delphic utterances, seemed to restore complete confidence to the hearts of the timid ones, and so in high feather and with large hopes we steamed out of the now moonlit harbor, out into the open sea.

During the afternoon I had seized the occasion to call upon our consul at St. Johns, Mr. Molloy, whom I found to be a very agreeable gentleman. He has been stationed at his present post for over twenty years, and has served longer than any other American consul. He had known all the Arctic explorers for the past quarter of a century, and had many interesting personal recollections. He told me that the famous explorer Hall, who at one time was supposed to have been poisoned by some of his crew, really died of eating too much cake. He was inordinately fond of cake, and ate three pounds of a rich compound one night—a feat that put a sudden end to his explorations.

As I was returning to the ship after my visit I was joined by a member of the Newfoundland Parliament, McGrath (pronounced McGraw) by name—a jovial, hearty-looking man, who came on board and entered into conversation at once with a party gathered there. When we explained our intention of entering Melville Bay he looked both surprised and amused. "Well, well," he remarked, "any one who would go to the Arctic regions for amusement would go to Sheol for recreation." Extremes sometimes meet, but though we came near it, perhaps, we did not finally find the Arctic regions a gateway to that eternally warm welcome we are told awaits the unregenerate.

Upon invitation I accompanied my new-found friend on shore again, and we spent some time in discussing the peculiar state of Newfoundland politics over an excellent bottle of port wine. Then we strolled through the main thoroughfare of St. Johns. A pretty girl in a pony-chaise drove by, and smiled upon us beamingly. My friend, who was deep in politics, did not observe; but I raised my hat and bowed. Then the M. P. looked at the retreating chaise, and eyed me inquiringly. "I am a worshipper of beauty," I explained; "I always bow to a pretty girl."

"Um," said he, "that was my wife."

On July 16, the day after leaving St. Johns, we passed a seemingly unending procession of icebergs, of all sizes and shapes. These at times assume most beautiful forms, and seem to build themselves better than they know. In particular, I shall never forget the striking beauty of one huge mass of ice that slowly passed us. In shape it resembled the ruins of some vast and magnificent cathedral, and a stately and perfect tower rose from the ruins and glinted and gleamed in the sun. It seemed as if some great Arctic Michael Angelo must have spent his life in giving shape and beauty to so grand a pile. The day was balmy and clear; a blue Italian sky hung above us, and it was a perfect delight to lie lazily in steamer-chairs upon the deck and with half-closed eyes dreamily watch the gleaming ghostly procession go by. One of our party counted one hundred and fifty icebergs that day. The summer of 1894 was especially prolific in icebergs. Wherever we touched in northern latitudes we were told that never had there been seen, within the memory of the oldest inhabitants, such vast quantities of ice. It is now generally understood by those who have studied far northern conditions that an unusually early prevalence of icebergs in low latitudes indicates a preceding hard winter in Arctic circles, and that the region of the northern ice-cap is particularly dangerous. Our own experiences, and the disasters that overtook Wellman and Jackson during the summer of 1894, all go to confirm this theory.

An iceberg at a convenient distance is a magnificent sight;

it is a thing of beauty that adds a real charm to the monotonous expanse of the sea; but distance lends enchantment to the view, as we discovered on the following morning.

It was foggy now, very foggy, and we were bowling along at a speed of about seven knots, on the morning of July 17. It was after breakfast, and a quarter after eight o'clock. I was standing on deck talking to Dr. Cook and Mr. Kersting, when suddenly the signal to reverse the engine was given. Simultaneously we looked forward, and through the dense fog there loomed an immense mass of ice directly ahead. It was too large a berg to give us time to clear it; there was nothing to be done but to strike it full and square. My eyes were fixed upon that great pile of ice with a strange fascination; there was hardly time to think or to have the feeling of fear communicated to the brain before, with a great crash, we struck the awful wall of ice before us. The iron prow of the ship ran right into the berg fully seven feet, and the ice, crumbling and breaking from the shock, fell in a great shower upon the forward deck. The reverse action of the propeller now began to draw us away from the berg, and the *Miranda* backed and careened to one side; there was a terrible moment of suspense, and then the vessel righted itself. A cry arose to lower the boats, and many rushed to get them in readiness. All this took less time than it takes to tell it. I had last seen my young charge, Carl Garrison, in our cabin, just forward of the dining-room, where he was engaged in cleaning his rifle—a favorite pastime of his on dull days, and one that brought to him dreams of the polar bear and the walrus that would fall by it later on. Naturally, I immediately went below to hunt for him, and as I passed through the dining-room I caught sight of Commodore Gardner coolly finishing his breakfast, as if unaware of the terrific shock that had made havoc with the plates and dishes. I caught sight of other forms also, rushing about in wild confusion. Captain Farrell came flying down and ordered all hands on deck. I passed quickly forward of the saloon to look for Carl, and was greatly relieved to find that no water was leaking in. Carl was not below, so I seized two overcoats from our cabin and speedily made my way on deck again, where I found my charge looking quite cool, as he had a right to look, being surrounded by a lot of broken ice. Indeed, there was no real panic, and for a lot of hitherto inexperienced Arctic explorers the party as a whole certainly behaved remarkably well. It was quickly

ICEBERG.

ascertained that notwithstanding the severity of the shock the damage that had been done was not so serious as to endanger the ship. This, of course, was a great relief to every one on board; for it would have been an inauspicious day to have taken to the boats, on account of the very heavy fog all around us. We had fortunately struck a projecting portion of the berg above our water-line, so that the blow came upon the upper starboard bow-plates; three of these were cracked or stove in, the hole running upward from about fifteen feet above the water-line. It was a great piece of luck that we did not strike the great mass of ice below the water which forms by far the greater part of an iceberg, the proportion of ice under the water to that above it being about eight to one. It was the projecting ice above that saved us from tearing out the bottom of the ship by striking the vast mass below; had we hit upon this, my readers would have been spared this narrative.

As the *Miranda* steamed cautiously forward again we passed close to the berg that had so nearly caused our ruin, and it certainly was an awe-inspiring mass of ice—perhaps a thousand feet in length and upward of two hundred feet high. We could see the hole that we had made, smeared as if with blood, from red paint about the prow of the *Miranda*. Slowly the great berg disappeared into the fog, which had somewhat lifted, and we were much relieved to get out of its dangerous proximity. There were plenty more of its companions, however, silently and slowly moving southward, so that a sharp lookout was kept as we went onward toward Cape Charles harbor, on the Labrador coast, about twenty-five miles away, and the nearest port to put in for repairs. A meeting of the passengers was called soon after the collision, and it was decided to put in to Cape Charles for repairs, and then continue on our journey. We reached Cape Charles early in the afternoon; but as we had a variety of experiences and adventures before we again put out from this port, it will be well to relate them in a succeeding chapter.

CHAPTER II.

It was early in the afternoon of July 17 that we steamed slowly into the harbor of Cape Charles, on the bleak coast of Labrador. High barren hills rose all around us, destitute of vegetation for the most part, except that here and there a kindly moss covered their nakedness; a few small houses of fishermen perched on rocks constituted the settlement. Not a very inviting shore, but still it was not long before we were upon it; for it was always a delight to leave the cramped quarters on our vessel and be able to stretch our legs with freedom. It did not take us long to form the acquaintance of most of the population of Cape Charles, because the population consists only of a half-dozen families, augmented somewhat in the fishing season by a few fishermen from Newfoundland. In the winter time the people literally take to the woods—that is, they retire into winter quarters in some woods about nine miles away. Very simple, very monotonous, and very dull is the life of a Labrador fisherman. He fishes and he eats and he sleeps, and that tells about the whole story. He is always in debt to the company that runs the fisheries, and so he can sell his fish only to the company, who take care to keep him in debt by charging him very high prices for his few necessaries of life. I sat frequently by the fireside of one family in particular, by the name of Pye, with whom I ingratiated myself by presenting

a few copies of old magazines, which I could see were highly
appreciated, for literature is very scarce at Cape Charles, and
these magazines will probably become family heirlooms.
From chatting with this family I learned that this is the *modus
vivendi* of the inhabitants of these regions: The men fish in
summer, of course, and in the fall they chop and saw wood, and

THE PYE FAMILY.

do odd jobs of various kinds in preparation for the rigors of the
winter; in winter they mend nets and boats, and thus prepare
for summer, or the fishing season, for there is no spring worth
speaking of; the ice blocks them until June. They hunt in
the winter also, and set their traps; and this is their chief excitement, as also their chief means for procuring food. The
principal game consists of rabbits, ptarmigan, spruce par-

tridges, porcupine, and deer. The men build little cabins about the deer-hunting grounds in the interior, and from them they will start out in the very early morning and hunt all day long, and tramp for forty or fifty miles over hills and gorges, carrying with them but the scantiest supply of food. They will sometimes remain in these cabins, and continue this sort of a life, despite all kinds of inclement weather, for a month at a time. Deer are not plentiful, and are hard to get, but the porcupine is found in greater numbers and is easily killed. The Canadian porcupine is an animal more or less peculiar to this region. It comes out of its hiding-places in winter and is easily tracked in the snow. Its food is the berry and the bark of trees, which it gnaws in such a manner as to be easily recognized by the hunter. When overtaken on the ground it rolls itself up in a ball and erects its spines for a defence; when pursued it shows great agility in taking to the tree-tops. The lives of the women, as is generally the case everywhere, are more monotonous and confined than those of the men. They stay at home and cook, and make all the clothes and boots. These latter are made of sealskin, and very good boots they are, too; and some of the women help in cleaning and preparing the fish, which are salted away in the storehouses. Of course, they do some fancy-work also. Is there a spot on the face of the globe where the women do not do fancy-work in some form or other? It is one of the prerogatives and a universal habit of the sex, and one deserving of every encouragement. Barren as are the interiors of the little houses in Labrador, they are still relieved by bits of color, which the women weave into appropriate forms. Hassocks, watch-cases, pouches, and cushions are the main forms that fancy-work takes in Labrador. The hassocks are a series of pockets made out of long strips of cloth and prettily set off with ribbons and beadwork in a variety of ways according to the taste of the maker. Of course, in so sparsely settled and busy a place there can be little

CAPE CHARLES.

general intercourse or social amusements. A dance takes place occasionally, and this is always a great event. We had a dance during our stay, which was quite a unique affair; but the native ladies were shy of dancing with us, and our dances were strange to them, so our mainstays were the two Eskimo girls, Mary and Clara, who were quite equal to the occasion, and enjoyed exceedingly being the belles of the ball. Our orchestra was the old man Peter, the father of the girls, who played the fiddle; so it was mainly the Eskimos who kept the ball rolling. We danced by the light of a few dim lanterns in a little storehouse whose floor was so slippery with codliver oil that we had to throw salt upon it to increase the friction, and enable us to retain our equilibrium. All the élite of Cape Charles attended, which added to the group of wallflowers very materially, and encroached upon the dancing space. It was a remarkable scene altogether, and our photographer, Mr. Kersting, took an excellent flash-light picture of it; but, alas! this, together with a vast number of other photographs, many of them of scenes and places never before seen by white men, went down with the unfortunate *Miranda*.

Of course, our vessel was an object of great interest to the Cape Charles people: so large a steamer had never been there before. We were as popular as a circus in the rural districts of the United States, and the men brought their wives and children over to look at the wonders of the ship, and to see the sheep on board—natural curiosities which were much admired and never before seen in that place. One old fellow was very much struck with the ice-water cooler; he thought it the most remarkable piece of mechanism that he had ever seen, and never tired of standing by it and watching people, as they drew a glass of water, with open-mouthed admiration.

There was always quite a collection of small fishing craft which kept in the neighborhood of the *Miranda*, in wait for any fishing parties that might be going out. It was difficult to know what to pay the fishermen for their services, as the general medium of exchange throughout Labrador is trade; money is seldom used, and its relative value is but dimly appreciated. As the natives do not know well the value of their own money, American money caused great confusion among them; they took it, but they could not distinguish denominations—a one-dollar bill meant as much to them as a ten.

Cod is the staple fish along the Labrador coast. They can be hauled up almost anywhere, and though a mess of fresh cod is by no means to be despised, still the catching of them is not very fascinating sport. We do not care for anything in life that is too easily acquired—and cod is so dead easy! However, the fishermen do not take this point of view—the easier the fishing, and the more that come to their nets, the merrier; and so cod is a very popular fish about Labrador. Indeed, in the local vernacular, cod alone is fish, salmon is salmon, herring is herring, and trout is trout; but cod is fish, and nothing else is called fish. Such is the devotion to cod at Cape Charles that the fishermen seem to swear by it, for I often heard them mutter something that sounded very much like "By Cod!"

But there is plenty of other sport besides cod-fishing. There is, I was informed, excellent duck-shooting all along the coast in the spring and autumn. Eider-ducks abound, as do guillemots, puffin, murres, and auks. These birds collect by the thousands, and will keep the sportsman just as busy as he pleases. In July, during our brief stay, we found the guillemot particularly abundant, and quite a number of these birds were bagged. It is a very pretty bird, a glossy black, with carmine legs and beak, but rather hard to kill, because it dives at the flash; it is very quick and nimble, and can swim a great distance under water. When hit, it does not give up the ghost easily, but will, unless struck in a vital part, dive, and often several charges will have to be pumped into it before it can be captured. On the wing, it flies rapidly, but low and straight. From behind a ledge in a neighborhood where these birds congregate, one can get excellent wing-shooting. Later on, we came across numbers of guillemot along the fiords of Greenland.

Once in a while in the winter a polar bear comes floating down to Cape Charles, and is sure to be given a warm reception. A splendid specimen kindly brought his skin down with him and left it on the Labrador coast in the winter of 1894. The entire male population turned out to greet him, and it was not long before poor bruin was overtaken, floundering about helplessly in the snow, and he was easily induced to part with his hide. Dr. Cook purchased the skin from one of the fishermen, and it is now hanging up in the fore-cabin of the *Miranda*, very safe from rats, but perhaps food for fishes.

Battle Harbor lies across the bay from Cape Charles, a distance of five or six miles. I could never get a satisfactory explanation of why it was called Battle Harbor, for several old inhabitants whom I interviewed all had different stories to tell, although they all agreed that a battle had been fought there in very early times. Some said the battle was between the English and Eskimos, others between the English and Indians, and still others held that the battle was fought between Indians and Eskimos. The settlement is a very important place, viewed from the Labrador standpoint; it contains about fifty houses, and a mail steamer calls every fortnight during the summer from St. Johns, Newfoundland. Like most of the Labrador settlements, its population consists principally of dogs. There are at least a dozen dogs to each family, and one cannot enter a house without walking over a number of them. Luckily, they are good-natured and kindly disposed toward strangers, as are their masters. We made up a small party and went over to Battle Harbor in a couple of lifeboats, rowing past some very interesting stranded icebergs on the way. With Dr. R. M. Cramer I subsequently rowed under one of these bergs, and though we got an ice-cold shower-bath from the constant drip overhead, we were well repaid. There were numerous caverns opening a few feet above the water, and into one of these we rowed. Its dome and sides were of a gorgeous blue, and the ice beneath the wonderfully clear water gleamed and glinted from below : it seemed like the entrance to a fairy structure, and we almost looked for a

A STRANDED BERG

mermaid to arise to guide us through the labyrinths of this wonderful ice-palace.

At Battle Harbor we were hospitably entertained by the agent of the owners of the fisheries, Mr. Hall, who introduced us to a favorite Labrador drink made from a mixture of spruce-beer and rum. Spruce-beer is a very popular drink in Labrador, and every well-regulated family keeps a supply on hand ; rum is also popular, but rarer.

There is a neat little hospital in the place, supported by the English Missions to the Deep Sea Fisheries; it is under the charge of a bright-faced young English nurse, who has a native assistant. A young doctor is sent over during the summer season, but returns to England for the winter. The brave young nurse stays all the year round, notwithstanding the rigors of the winter season, and acts the part of both nurse and doctor during the long months when the ice has cut off all communication with the outer world. A few of us greatly enjoyed an impromptu afternoon tea gotten up for us by the nurse, in which the doctor participated; indeed, we were entertained by an angel unawares, for some staunch hot buns and comfortable sandwiches that we ate stood us in lieu of the dinner we expected to have on the *Miranda;* for it was many hours before we tasted food again. This was the reason: When we started on the return trip the wind was so strong, and the waves were running so high, that we decided to skirt around some islands and to get back to the ship by a much longer but more sheltered route.

THE DESERT ISLAND.

"The longest way round is the shortest way home," says an old saw; but I have never known it to work. After rowing for miles, with the waves dashing over us every now and then, we found it impossible to make any headway against wind and tide in trying to round a point, and were obliged to put in to shore upon a desert island—a bleak and barren spot, offering but little shelter. We gathered some scrubby underbrush, however, and stretched ourselves, thoroughly tired out with our struggles with wind and wave and oar, around the fire that we built. Spasmodic attempts were made to keep up a cheerful conversation; but as there was nothing to eat or drink, and as most of us were pretty well drenched, it would have taxed Mark Tapley himself to have kept up an appearance of jollity. There was a sense of desolateness about the place hard to describe, while the wind moaned dismally over it.

> "—A wind that shrills
> Over a waste land, where no one comes,
> Or has come since the making of the world."

The moon rose cold and clear, and looked down upon a dejected and shivering group huddled around a flickering fire. It was cold, very cold, and the wind still blew, and the great waves dashed against the rocky shore. At length, some time after midnight, there came a lull in the tempest, and we gladly took to our boats again. It was a long, hard pull against wind and tide; but very beautiful seemed the barren, rocky islands in the now bright moonlight, and the sky up above was a wonder and a revelation, with the great northern lights ever and anon streaming over it, then dimming and dying, then flashing out again in long, shining clouds that lit up earth and sky. It was three o'clock in the morning before we reached our home on the rolling deep, and never did the *Miranda's* lights seem more welcome to us than when they gleamed over the waters in the gray dawn of that morning.

Later on that day, July 21, a communication from Captain Farrell was read by Dr. Cook to the assembled members of the expedition. This stated that it would be necessary to return to St. Johns, Newfoundland, for more permanent repairs. Temporary repairs had been completed, but as there were no extra plates on board, nor any way of procuring such, the engineers had cut a plate from the iron protection surrounding the forward hatch, between the upper and main decks; but as tools were lacking to cut this plate properly, it so covered the hawser pipe as to render the starboard anchor unavailable. Therefore, Captain Farrell deemed it unsafe to proceed northward, and there was nothing to be done but to beat a retreat to St. Johns and remain there until satisfactory repairs could be completed. This was very discouraging to all; but we had to bow to the inevitable.

Five of our party had already made up their minds to give up the trip, and had started on a hunting jaunt toward the interior of Labrador. These were the Messrs. C. P. and T. J. Lineaweaver, and R. DeP. Tytus, of Yale College; Walter S. Root, of Cleveland, Ohio, and S. G. Tenney, of Williamstown, Mass. The party camped in the Labrador woods for seventeen days, and enjoyed excellent sport both with gun and rod. They captured one bear and several lynxes, and shot great quantities of grouse and other small game. One of the party, Mr. Tytus, had quite an experience with a lynx. He shot it and thought that it was dead, but on approaching the supposed corpse the lynx suddenly sprang upon him and tore his clothes to shreds before it received its final *coup de grâce*. On their return along the coast the party shot a number of seal and guillemots. In the Labrador streams they found trout and salmon,—trout exceedingly plentiful,—and caught them in such quantities that, as one of the party said to me on a chance meeting in New York, "We are afraid to talk in figures—everybody would think we were simply telling fish stories."

One discomfort of the short summer season in Labrador is the extraordinary variations of temperature. The party

A HUNTING PARTY.

had a thermometer with them, which would stand at perhaps below the freezing-point early in the morning, but by high noon the mercury sometimes mounted upward of a hundred degrees in the sun. None of the party, however, suffered any ill effects. They enjoyed perfect health, and were greatly pleased with their outing.

On the evening of July 21 Professor Hite and his party, consisting of Messrs. Howard Bucknell, George M. Coates, and G. H. Perkins, of Philadelphia, left the ship to start upon their journey into the interior of Labrador. Professor Hite's original intention had been to land in the neighborhood of Rigolette, but the iceberg incident caused him to make a change of plan. As the small party of explorers rowed away from the ship in two little skiffs, towing their tents and provisions in tenders behind them, they were given three rousing cheers.

The party made their way to Independent Harbor on the regular mail-boat which runs during the summer from Cape Charles. From there they secured passage in a small boat to Separation Point, a narrow point of land separating the White Bear from the Eagle River. Here a cache was made for provisions, and the party started to explore the White Bear River. On the second day they came to a cataract sixty feet in height. Mr. Bucknell had been taken quite ill, so a camp was pitched at the foot of the falls, and he was left in the care of Mr. Coates, while Professor Hite and Mr. Perkins continued the exploration of the river, which they ascended a distance of nearly two hundred miles from its mouth. The river terminated in a chain of small lakes. Upon returning to the camp Mr. Bucknell's condition had not improved, and he was sent over to Cartwright, the most southern and eastern Hudson Bay trading-post on the Labrador shore. The other members of the party then continued the exploration of the Eagle and Paradise rivers. On the banks of the Paradise

River they found an abundance of plants not noted in the more mountainous districts, and they also came across a great many species of water-birds. They procured a number of seal along this river, and found abundance of trout. On the north side of Sandwich Bay, on a mountain nineteen hundred feet in height, quite a number of caribou were seen, and some of them secured. The party obtained in all thirty-nine species of mammals and seventy-seven species of birds, all of which, with the exception of two, are listed by Professor Packard in his work "The Labrador Coast." Mr. Coates made a large collection of plants, and five species of butterflies not mentioned by Professor Packard were procured. The party left Cartwright on September 14 for Pilley's Island, off the Newfoundland coast, and there caught the steamer *Sylvia* for New York, where they arrived on September 30, very nearly three months from the date of the start.

The party of Eskimos also left us to take the mail steamer at Battle Harbor and go onward to Rigolette; and still another party silently stole away in the small hours of the morning. This was composed of Robert D. Perry, of Phillipston, Mass.; William Bryce, Jr., of New York, and Dr. Willis A. Reeve, of Patchogue, L. I. These three men suddenly made up their minds that night to take the bird in the hand, and make sure of some hunting in Labrador, rather than take the risk of being dry-docked in St. Johns. They pushed their way onward toward Rigolette, enjoyed some excellent sport in this vicinity, and got safely back to New York somewhat in advance of the party they had left behind.

A heavy fog had closed about the *Miranda*, but early in the morning of the 22d it lifted sufficiently to enable the ship to start on its retreat to St. Johns. All day long, however, progress was very slow; for the fog descended again like a curtain, and now and then the ghostly shapes of huge icebergs could be dimly discerned. The passengers made up a watch among themselves that night to supplement the regular watch. It fell to my lot to watch from two till three in the morning. This was one of the longest hours I ever spent, on account of the dull monotony of straining the eyes to seaward and seeing nothing; not an iceberg loomed in sight.

ICEBERG.

Once, when the fog had lifted a trifle, some commotion was excited by the sailor who was on watch with me singing out: "A light on the starboard bow!" Immediately the fog-whistle was set to blowing, and Mr. Dumphy, the ice-pilot, came rushing forward. "Where's the light?" said he. "Over there," said the sailor. "Humph!" said Pilot Dumphy, after gazing intently for a minute or so, "that's nothing but a star," and he went back to his perch by the wheel-house much disgruntled.

Later in the day the fog lifted entirely, and we were enabled to proceed at full speed. We passed many icebergs on the way, and by midnight we were once more anchored safe and sound in the landlocked harbor of St. Johns.

CHAPTER III.

It seemed like an old story to be back at St. Johns again, for though we had stopped there but a few hours when going to the northward, yet both harbor and city are apt to impress themselves upon one at a glance and to remain fixed in one's memory. Of course, our second arrival created no little excitement, especially after the news of the collision with the iceberg had circulated through the town, and the prophets gathered about us and reminded us of their warnings. The realization of a dire prophecy is the greatest happiness that can come to the heart of a prophet, and so our return brought exceeding great joy to several of the local seers.

As we knew that we were in for a stay of several days, we proceeded to enjoy ourselves as much as possible, and were aided and abetted in these efforts by a number of the kind and hospitable citizens of St. Johns. The doors of the City Club—the principal social club—were thrown open to us, and this became a headquarters and general meeting-place for the members of the expedition. Here were fine, large reading-rooms, in which we found all the leading American magazines and papers, a beautiful billiard-room, and an excellent *café*. Those only who have been cooped up in the narrow confines of a ship can appreciate the comfort that such a club can bring.

St. Johns is a capital place to spend the midsummer in. It is cool and pleasant, and has charming surroundings.

Within its confines is a fine sheet of fresh water; Quidi Vidi Lake it is called, or rather it is spelled that way, and commonly called Kitty Viddy. The lake is admirably adapted for aquatic sports, and here annual regattas take place in the month of August, and are, I am told, very exciting affairs, attended by the entire population.

ON THE ROAD TO TOPSAIL.

About a dozen miles from St. Johns is one of the most charming resorts that it has ever been my good fortune to visit. It is known as Topsail Beach. There are no large hotels there—in fact, no hotels at all, but only several small but neat and pretty inns, or boarding-houses; for Topsail yet awaits the magic touch of capital to broadly popularize it. As it is, nature has been very lavish to the place, and its situation and the country surrounding it are very beautiful. I ran out there one fine Saturday afternoon with Professor Freeman, under the escort of Mr. McGrath, the bright young editor of the St. Johns *Herald,* who gave us much information about Newfoundland in general on the way. The train was crowded with excursionists running out for an afternoon's or a Sunday's outing; and a very bright, healthy, happy-looking lot of people they were. The ride afforded us many pretty glimpses of lake and woodland, but these were to be eclipsed by the first view of Topsail. It is situated on a magnificent bay called Conception, so named by the pious Portuguese navigator, Gaspar Cortereal, in the year 1500—a beautiful sheet of water gently rolling in upon a pebbly beach. The surrounding country is wild and rugged, and the combination of hills and forests and sea makes up an ideal resort, whether one wishes merely to loaf and enjoy his soul, or to hunt in the woodlands, or fish upon the sea. We took supper at one of the little inns, which had a number of small dining-rooms, so that parties could sup together without intrusion, and after enjoying a very comfortable and cozy meal we returned to St. Johns exceedingly pleased with our trip.

Indeed, I found the surroundings of St. Johns so very attractive that I much regretted I could not run farther into the interior, where many beautiful spots are to be found, and which is a paradise for the sportsman. But day and night the workmen were hammering away at the *Miranda's* bow, and it was only a question of a few days before she would be ready to start again on her northward journey.

The interior of Newfoundland has never yet been fully explored; and in the dense forests that dot it, as well as in the more open country, an abundance of game is to be found. In 1822 a Scotchman named Cormack crossed the island from east to west at its broadest point, but his journey has never been repeated. It is said that great numbers of caribou and

moose are to be found in the interior, while the countless
lakes and ponds abound with trout, and are the abodes of
wild geese, duck, and other fresh-water fowl. Beaver and
otter also dwell in these lonely lakes. Ptarmigan, curlew,
plover, and snipe are found all over the island, on the great
barrens or in the marshy grounds, and Arctic hare and rabbits also abound.

Of course, the cod is the great fish about Newfoundland,
for here are the greatest cod fisheries in the world ; the fisheries off the Labrador coast are controlled by Newfoundland,
as the territory is under the jurisdiction of the latter.
The second great industry of the island is the seal fishery,
the products derived therefrom forming about one-eighth
of its entire exports. In olden times this industry was
carried on solely by sailing vessels and boats, but about thirty
years ago steam sealers were introduced ; and these, of course,
have a decided advantage over sailing craft. They are power-
fully built, to withstand the pressure of the ice, and are large
enough to carry from a hundred to three hundred men ; but
the men are crowded into very close quarters. The risks of the
voyage, the adventures in catching seals, and the large gains to
be derived thereby, attract numbers of volunteers, and of these
the steamers have the pick. On account of the ice, the law
does not allow the sealers to clear before March 10, and
the season lasts but six weeks. It is a common thing for a
steamer to return in three or four weeks, laden down with
thirty or forty thousand seals, worth from two to three
dollars apiece. A third of the proceeds is divided among the
men ; the captain gets so many cents per seal, and the
remainder goes to the owner of the vessel. Lying about us
were quite a fleet of these steam sealers.

The conviction had forced itself upon us that the *Miranda*
was "not the man for Galway," was not the ship fitted for
ice-service. It was a question as to whether we could pro-

ceed with any degree of safety; and we were obliged, much to our disappointment, to give up all thought of entering Melville Bay, both on account of the delay we had experienced and the danger of getting nipped by pack ice, for every one said that in such a contingency the *Miranda* would be crushed like an egg-shell. After considerable deliberation and consulting of authorities, it was decided that it would be safe for us to proceed to the southern coast of Greenland; for, by taking the right course, there would be little danger of meeting much ice at this time of year. Notwithstanding the opinion of authorities, however, the people in general looked upon us as little less than crazy for attempting to go on at all after our unfortunate experience.

A small party of our excursionists were skirting about the suburbs of the town one morning, when they came across the lunatic asylum, and thought they would like to inspect it. They rang the bell, and the door was opened by an attendant, who said that visitors were not admitted upon that day. "We come from the *Miranda*," said one of the party, starting to explain. "Oh, walk right in!" immediately responded the attendant, and the door was opened wide. The party entered, but with an uncanny feeling that the heavy door might close upon them and bid them leave all hope behind. Meantime, the hammers were drumming merrily on the *Miranda* night and day at her wharf close by the great dry-dock at St. Johns. This is one of the largest dry-docks in the world. There were three vessels getting repaired in it while we lay by. It was erected at a cost of $600,000. It had been dredged out, and its sides were heavily timbered in steps. The vessels sail in, and then the entrance is closed by a pontoon-gate. The water is pumped out by pumps so large and powerful that they will empty the basin within four hours.

On July 28 the hammering ceased, the repairs were completed, and we started for Frederickshaab, South Greenland, planning to go directly across the straits, and thus avoid the Labrador coast and its numerous icebergs. We started at about nine o'clock in the evening, but anchored after steaming out a little way, and did not get well under way until five o'clock on the following morning. The day was foggy at first, but the fog lifted, and we bowled merrily along, making good

THE MIRANDA IN DOCK.

time, and with everybody in high spirits. Shortly after breakfast we passed Baccalieu Island, which is most densely populated by seagulls. A few shots fired from the ship echoed and reverberated about the island, and caused a partial eclipse of the sun, on account of the dense mass of gulls that circled over us. Not until I saw the wonderful loomeries of

Greenland did I behold again such countless myriads of gulls. This island is the farthest point out between Conception and Trinity bays. By the afternoon the coast had become a dim outline, and was soon lost to sight. We passed several magnificent icebergs—great, gleaming masses of ice, each of which on land would have covered acres of ground. The ship danced up and down, tossed by billows; but these great icebergs, sinking as they do so far and deep into the sea, are not moved by the motions of the surface, and the waves dash against them as against a rocky coast, and fall back again unheeded. The Arctic explorer Hayes says of icebergs: "The iceberg is the largest independent floating body in the universe except the heavenly orbs. There is nothing approaching it within the range of our knowledge on this globe of ours; and yet it is but a fragment of the ice-stream, which in turn is but an arm of the great ice-sea. And yet the iceberg is to the Greenland ice as the paring of a finger-nail to the human body, as a small chip to the largest oak, as a shovel of earth to Manhattan Island." This gives some faint idea of the vast amount of ice in the frozen regions of the North; the huge icebergs that passed us were but as little chips floating away from the great body of ice they had left behind.

For the first two or three days after leaving St. Johns we had fairly clear weather, and made good progress, and then a dense fog fell upon us. Day after day we drifted about without anybody knowing exactly where we were, for no accurate observations could be taken. Sometimes the fog would lift to reveal to us that we were surrounded by floe ice and icebergs. For days we coasted along this ice in fog and rain, attempting to find a passage through it. The long stretches of ice, and the large icebergs towering like mountains above, and the roaring of the waves dashing against the ice-floe, combined to make a scene both impressive and awful. The fog was very moist, and wet us like rain, great drops of water falling from it; and it grew very cold.

> " And now there came both mist and snow,
>   And it grew wondrous cold:
> And ice mast high came floating by,
>   As green as emerald.

> " The ice was here, the ice was there,
>   The ice was all around:
> It cracked and growled, and roared and howled
>   Like noises in a swound."

We first saw the Greenland coast early in the morning of August 3. The lofty peaks of Mount Nautsarsorfike and Mount Kunguat could be discerned, and were perhaps sixty or seventy miles distant. There was a great deal of floe ice between us and the land, and also on the west of us. Ice-pilot Dumphy wished to run through this ice; but Captain Farrell would not hear of it, and we slowly steamed westward to make a detour amid numberless pieces of broken ice. As we looked outward the ice seemed to form a continuous line along the horizon. Then the

THE GREENLAND COAST.

fog, seemingly more dense and heavy than ever, closed all about us, and the ship was obliged to lie to with the ice all around it. To the west of us there was a continuous roar as of waves beating upon a rocky shore, but it was the noise of the ice-pack. The water was very still, scarcely a ripple on its surface; and some of the men took advantage of the calm by going out in a small boat and securing a lot of ice from a wasted berg near the ship. They lassoed great pieces of ice, and in this way got about a ton on board.

At about six o'clock the fog cleared and disclosed an interesting state of affairs, for the floe was closing in on us. To the west of us was a line of pack ice like a wall, only about half a mile away; it stretched both ways as far as the eye could see, while to the east of us was another wall of ice, not

FLOE ICE.

so sharply defined, but too much of it to attempt a passage through. The *Miranda* fled in a southeasterly direction, and it was a most interesting retreat through shapes and forms of ice of all varieties and colors. Blue and green ice we saw of different shades, and sometimes ice tinted with red. The varying shapes kept us constantly interested, and the forms assumed at times by the ice were wonderfully beautiful and delicate. Here and there we saw seals, seated on masses of ice, who eyed us with evident curiosity, and occasionally a whale rose and spouted near the ship. Ice-pilot Dumphy was perched in the shrouds, and reported open places visible in a westerly direction. Slowly the ship picked its way through the ice-belt, and by half-past seven we got through the floe and into clear water, leaving a long line of ice behind.

It was now decided to run up to Disco, rather than try to get in at Frederickshaab. But again the fog fell around us on the ensuing day, and we drifted about, making little progress. We were in latitude 62° 50', and longitude 53° 49'. Whenever the fog lifted we could see icebergs about us—which made the captain very careful; and for some days we kept drifting about, mostly in fog so dense that no observations could be taken. On the morning of August 7, to our surprise and joy, we discovered that we were in sight of land— rugged and uninviting, to be sure, but still land. High mountains, with towering peaks covered with snow, and bleak and barren islands, were outlined in the distance. There was but little ice in sight, and we headed for the shore, with our whistle blowing to attract the attention of any inhabitants, should there prove to be a settlement upon this coast. For an hour or so we lay to, blowing our whistle and firing the cannon. After a while two little specks were seen afar off, and ere long were made out to be Eskimo kayaks. Before long a large boat hove in sight, and made directly for the ship. Soon it was alongside of us, and proved to contain several Eskimos, who came on board and piloted our vessel into a snug little harbor surrounded by islands. Here was a settlement, and on a hill we saw a flagstaff flying the Danish flag, and collected about it a crowd of Eskimos, men and women— mostly the latter, who apparently were in a great state of excitement, and were looking down at us with every indication of curiosity and interest. Little houses or igloos were perched about on the rocky hills, and near the landing was the more commodious house of the Danish governors. The place proved to be Sukkertoppen (Sugar-loaf), an Eskimo settlement of about four hundred people, ruled by Governor Bistrup and Assistant Governor Baumann. As soon as the ship dropped anchor we were surrounded by a fleet of kayaks and oomiaks—

DANISH BUILDINGS AT SUKKERTOPPEN.

or woman's boat. It was not long before several of our boats were lowered among this, to us, novel fleet, and we were soon on shore. Here the entire population, with the exception of those in the boats, had gathered just in front of the governors' house, and received us with every expression of simple-minded wonder and delight. We found that the governors were away for the time being, and so we paid our respects to their ladies, and were most hospitably entertained by them. After coming out from the governors' house we had great sport with the natives. The prettiest girls were selected from the crowd, which kept in a solid phalanx, and induced, with much difficulty at times, for they were not lacking in coquetry, to come forward and have their pictures taken. Then we scattered over the settlement generally, and the crowd broke and followed us about in sections.

It was not long before the commercial spirit displayed

THE LADIES RECEIVE US.

itself on both sides, and many of our party went back to the ship to gather trading material which they had brought with them. They came back bearing bags of every description filled with knickknacks and old clothes. The place looked as if it were being overrun with Hebrew peddlers, and the scene was comical in the extreme. Some stood up on rocks, surrounded by an excited crowd of Eskimos, mostly women, and auctioned their goods to the highest bidders, or to those who displayed the articles they wished, while others made a regular house-to-house canvass, and had great times dickering with the residents thereof ; for bargaining had to be carried on by signs not always rightly interpreted. Such a babel of tongues as arose, such shouts of laughter, had probably never before been heard in Sukkertoppen. One of our party, who had read Mark Twain's story of the "Eskimo Maiden's Romance," had purchased a supply of twenty-five hundred large and shining fish-hooks with which to dazzle the eyes of the natives: nay, he thought almost to blind them with his display of wealth. But alas for him, fish-hooks seemed to be a drug on the market in this particular settlement, and though he pulled whole handfuls of them out from his bag, he produced no curiosity or interest. Now I had been led to believe by several Arctic explorers whom I had questioned before starting that nothing was dearer to the heart of the Eskimo than a needle, and the bigger the better. Consequently, I had purchased a lot of needles so large that as I carried them through New York I was in fear of being arrested for carrying concealed deadly weapons ; but thoughts of the fine lot of furs I should bring back in exchange consoled me for the risk. I hummed to myself the song of the magnet in "Patience," slightly altered to suit the occasion :

> "For if I can wheedle
> A knife or a needle,
> O why not an Eskimo?"

But needles attracted no more attention among the inhabitants of Sukkertoppen than did fish-hooks. Some knowing ones had probably been here before us and flooded the market. Ribbons were the things that went like hot cakes, and a man with enough ribbons could soon have owned the town. All the women wore ribbons in their hair, which was tied up in a top-knot. These ribbons were worn not only for ornament, but also to designate the lady's condition. Maids wore red, married women blue, widows black, and those who were neither maid, wife, nor widow, green. Some of the widows wore black and red ribbons interlaced; these formed a sort of quick or the dead colors, and indicated a willingness to marry again. It chanced that a young theological student of our party had brought with him a great roll of green ribbon, and when he saw how popular ribbons appeared to be, he brought forth his roll and unwound it before a lot of maidens and their mammas. The hilarity that he produced embarrassed him, and when he attempted to hand his ribbons for examination to any one of them the manner in which they ran laughing from him embarrassed him all the more, and filled him with astonishment. Never-

ESKIMO BELLE.

theless, he persevered, and produced his ribbons in the midst of many a virtuous household. But when an ethnologist of the party, learned in Eskimo lore, explained to him the significance of the wearing of the green, he immediately returned to the *Miranda,* where he might blush unseen.

A JUVENILE.

While the green ribbon does not render its wearer a social pariah and outcast, as did the flaming scarlet letter in the days of the Puritans, still on the other hand it is not a badge of social distinction, and its wearers are not regarded as the leaders of Sukkertoppen's "four hundred." But then there are no social leaders in this primitive settlement, and no color line is drawn ; so blue ribbon and green ribbon and red ribbon and black ribbon mingled together without thought of caste.

Men and women dress so much alike that, were it not for the top-knots and ribbons of the gentler sex, it would be hard to distinguish them. The upper garment is a "timiak"—a vest of birdskin—and over this is worn a kind of cotton jersey called "anorak." On the legs are worn breeches of sealskin or of reindeer skin. The women's breeches are shorter than the men's, but to make up for this they wear longer boots, called "kamics," which reach above the knee. The men's kamics go but little above the ankle. There is also more ornamentation about the dress of the women. Their breeches are richly decorated in front with colored skin and white strips of dog or reindeer skin, and their long kamics are brightly colored, and the fronts of these are also decorated with stripes. Indeed, the costumes are very picturesque, and vastly more becoming to these people than the ugly garments that civilization has forced upon us.

By the afternoon the *Miranda* looked like a floating museum of natural history. There were already a considerable collection of stuffed birds on board, which had been prepared by the naturalists of the expedition; then a number of stuffed seals had been secured in St. Johns, and a variety of skins in Labrador. This collection was now augmented by all kinds of Eskimo goods in the way of costumes,

PORTRAIT OF A LADY.

boots, fur slippers, ornaments, implements of the chase, and kayaks. Sixteen of these wonderful little boats now adorned the decks of the *Miranda*. The kayak is an ingenious evolution from the birch-bark canoe of the North American Indian, and is remarkably well adapted to the uses required of it. It is built of a frame of wood or bone, about twenty feet in length and two and a half in breadth. A covering of sealskin, perfectly water-proof, is tightly stretched over the frame, and in the middle of the

THE KAYAK.

top there is a hole just large enough to permit the kayaker to get his body in and take his seat on the bottom of the boat with his legs stretched out in front of him. He wears a sealskin coat with a hood over his head, and the coat fits tightly around a rim round the aperture of the kayak, so that it is impossible for any water to get into the boat. A double paddle flaring at both ends is used, and the kayak is sent over the water with great swiftness. It is wonderful to see these little fellows go skimming over the water in their canoes. They can perform all kinds of antics with the ease of an acrobat, and are rather fond of showing off their skill. They can turn complete somersaults in the water, turning over and righting themselves with the greatest ease; and another form of sport is to spurt the boat forward and to jump completely over the bow of another boat. In these little canoes they hunt the seal and walrus, and all game to be found above or under the water, and the boats are equipped with various ingenious implements of the chase. There are different kinds of fishing tackle, and a bird-spear of wood, pointed with a bone spear-head, and a circle of barbed bone lance-heads contrived so as to give a whirling motion to the spear and thus entangle the object at which it is thrown. Then there is a harpoon for seals, so arranged with a joint that after the spear-head has struck the animal it becomes detached from the shaft, the head being connected with a thong in the hands of the hunter. This thong is attached to a float consisting of a large bladder or an inflated and air-tight

ESKIMOS AT PLAY.

skin, which prevents the escape or sinking of the wounded animal.

Indeed, the Eskimos show considerable inventive genius and skill in the construction of such articles as are needed in their grim struggle for existence in an environment unfavorable to human life. They will hold their own with any aboriginal race on the face of the globe. Our civilization cannot help them in so far as their struggle for life in their environment is concerned. With their iron implements they can secure all necessary food ; the possession of fire-arms only leads to wanton destruction, and to the frightening away of the game that is most precious to them. Their clothes, certainly, are better adapted to their climate than any we could make for them, and our most skilful boat-builders could not build them boats that would serve them as well as those they build for themselves.

The importation of various European products has undoubtedly worked harm among these now semi-civilized Eskimos. They have acquired a taste for tobacco, coffee, European fabrics, and various knickknacks. In exchange for these doubtful commodities they give their necessities of life—sealskin and blubber. Their boats and tents—absolute necessities—go to rack and ruin, unless the necessary sealskin is forthcoming; and in winter without blubber they lack both light and warmth. They are an improvident people, and

ESKIMO HOUSE.

will exchange during their brief summer, for luxuries to them, such as coffee and tobacco, things that are absolute necessities during their long winters, and so entail upon themselves the severest suffering—even starvation and death. They especially delight in coffee and tobacco, both of which are deleterious to them. The coffee they drink very strong, and they revel in the brief exhilaration that it affords them. But they are aware of its injurious effects, and young men who are destined to be good seal-catchers are allowed little or none. It is apt to produce a giddiness fatal to a kayaker, who needs to have always a clear head. They both chew and smoke tobacco, and even the little children will run after you—girls as well as boys—begging for some of the precious weed. Spirits are not allowed by the Danish governors to be sold or exchanged among them; but if by any means they can procure any, they delight in the effects produced. Nansen, the Arctic explorer, says, in speaking of these West Greenland Eskimos: "They are passionately fond of spirits, men and women alike—not because they like the taste, as I was often told, but because it is so delightful to be drunk. And drunk they become at every possible opportunity. Somewhat incongruously, too, the women, as a rule, like their husbands best when they are in a state of intoxication."

MOTHER AND BABE.

Living on the verge of existence, these people have need of all their natural powers in their grim battle with an inimical and difficult environment. The few virtues of civilization that are with difficulty grafted upon them hardly compensate for the civilized vices, which are only too easily spread among them, and which so weaken them in their hard struggle for existence.

Indeed, the Danish Government has recognized the fact that intercourse with civilized people is positively detrimental to the Eskimos, and so it prohibits civilized persons other than officials of the Government from remaining for any length of time among them. Professor Dyche, of our party, the well-known naturalist and hunter, wished to remain in Greenland all the winter, in order to increase his already great collection of North American mammals; but he was informed that he could not remain without a permit from the Danish Government. Nothing daunted, he secured a permit after his return to this country, and started again for Greenland in a small schooner the following spring. At Holsteinborg he connected with the Peary Relief Expedition, and returned with it, bringing with him nearly 4,000 specimens of Arctic birds, eggs, and animals. This is the largest collection that has ever been made in the Arctic regions, and as it was made within four months, great credit must be given Professor Dyche for his energy and brilliant work.

As it was decided to remain at Sukkertoppen for a couple of days, a party under Professor Wright was organized to visit and explore a glacier about thirty miles away, up a fiord called Isortok. Toward evening we started off in two boats, a lifeboat and a dory. In the lifeboat were Professors Wright and Jillson, Messrs. Dove, Kersting, Frederick Wright, Jr., Dunning, myself, and three Eskimos. In the dory were Messrs. Ladd, Rogers, Carpenter, Joyner, and one Eskimo. The Eskimos are good and untiring oarsmen. They row a slow stroke, but they put their muscle into it and make it tell. We took turns at the stroke oar, and occasionally spelled the Eskimos; but not often, for they can row for hours on a stretch, and at the end seem as fresh as at the commencement. It was a beautiful row, amid strange and novel scenery. When we were well out at sea, the sun, now a fiery red ball, sank behind the great snow-capped mountains, tinting them and the clouds above with streaks of purple and gold—tints that the waters reflected. Then we entered narrow and winding channels, and rowed in and out among a

FIRST CAMP IN GREENLAND.

number of small islands, mere rocks and moss, as desolate and forbidding as could well be imagined. There is a vast, brooding silence which hangs over the great wastes of Greenland; it seems almost like an impertinence to break it, by even the dip of an oar, while the sound of laughter or of a human voice seems strangely and weirdly out of place. In the long Arctic twilight we rowed for many hours, until at length we entered the Isortok fiord, and near the mouth of this we pitched our camp for the night. It was our first camp in Greenland, and it was called Camp Outing.

We were up betimes in the morning, and immediately after breakfast started for the glacier. The mainland was on our right, a continuous stretch of steep declivities and towering mountains. As we turned a bend we could see afar off the white line of the glacier coming down from on high to the water's edge. It was hours before we reached it, however, for it was many miles away. Once we met an oomiak, escorted by a couple of kayaks. It was a party of Eskimos, men and women, returning from fishing. We stopped and exchanged greetings, and also exchanged a couple of plugs of tobacco and a mouth-organ for some very fine salmon. The Eskimos went on their way rejoicing, and with a concourse of sweet sounds that were emitted vigorously from the mouth-organ. They probably thought us very simple people to part with so rare and wonderful an instrument for just a mess of fish.

FRONT VIEW OF THE ISORTOK GLACIER.

We reached the glacier finally at about noon, and it was not long before we were scaling up the steep mountain-sides, following the course of the glacier upward. It was like climbing the Alps, where "peaks on peaks arise," and none of us were able to reach the top—our time was too limited. I clambered with Mr. Ladd to an altitude of about twenty-five hundred feet, from whence we enjoyed a magnificent view of the numerous islands and fiords that lay below, of the mainland of Greenland, and of the great ocean beyond. Twice we crossed spurs of the glacier, and our feet sank deep in the soft snow; for the sun was so hot that we partially stripped ourselves during our ascent. The moss that for the most part covered the rocks was green and beautiful, and scattered about in rich profusion were great numbers of wild flowers gorgeous in their hues. The glaciers are the mothers of icebergs, which are not formed of ice frozen on the surface of the polar seas, but are pieces broken from the sea-ends of Arctic glaciers. The interior of Greenland is covered with a vast ice-cap, from which, down the valleys that extend between the central tableland to the Atlantic on the east and Baffin's Bay on the west, the ice glides down in frozen streams resistlessly to the sea. During the brief Arctic summer the action of the waves upon the debouching mouths of these great frozen rivers, aided by the unwonted warmth of the sun, detaches hundreds of thousands of tons of ice from the great glaciers, and thus icebergs are launched upon their career. This breaking off of icebergs from the parent glacier is called calving, owing to a fancied resemblance between the thunderous groans that accompany the process to the moaning of a cow in travail.

By six o'clock we were gathered at the foot of the steep mountains, and after a hasty meal started at once for a thirty-mile pull back to the ship.

After we were out of the fiord we encountered a heavy sea; as the wind was dead against us, we had a hard pull until we got in the lee of some islands, and the day was breaking before we got back to the *Miranda*.

A few hours later we started away from Sukkertoppen for Disco. Thoroughly tired out after our long pull, I was sleeping heavily, but was awakened by the noise of the moving ship. From out my port-hole I could see quite a fleet of kayaks about us, which raced along, keeping pace with the ship. A high sea was running, and the little boats would sometimes be hidden from sight in the trough, but only to rise

CREVASSE.

again in an instant on the crest of a wave, down which they would shoot like a toboggan. Gradually, the kayaks dropped away one by one, and still feeling stiff and sore from the exertions of the preceding day, I lay down in my bunk again and dropped off in a half-doze.

Suddenly there was an ominous and grating sound, and

we commenced to bump and jar in a most alarming manner.
I jumped to my feet, but was immediately thrown down, and
there was a great crash of breaking glass and china, and a
terrible ripping sound, as if the vessel were being torn asunder.
Men, furniture, and everything loose about the ship were
thrown about in the wildest confusion. For a moment we
seemed to be impaled upon the rocks, upon which we had
rushed with such terrific force, with our engines at full speed.
I dressed hastily and went on deck, where there was a scene
of great confusion. We had struck upon a hidden reef, but
with the high waves and the fast rate of speed at which
we were going we had managed to run over it and get clear.
Nobody could tell the extent of damage done, and so the
worst was prepared for. We felt that we were liable to sink
at any moment, and all knew that the rocks had gored our
vessel in a terrible manner. Many were pushing about with
life-preservers in their hands; some were working at the boats
to get them lowered, and others were bringing their most
valuable possessions up from their cabins to the deck. I saw
some strange sights: one man in his night-shirt, with a gun
in one hand and a life-preserver in the other, for some of the
passengers snatched at all sorts of odd things in the excitement of the moment; another man had the ship's cat pressed
against his bosom. The captain was cool and collected, and
giving his orders with sharp decision. Our whistles were
kept blowing continually, and our solitary cannon was fired
off at rapid intervals as we turned back and made for Sukkertoppen with all possible speed. It took some time to find out
whether we were leaking badly or not; then it was discovered
that the after water-ballast tank was full of water, but
as our pumps appeared able to keep the leakage from
gaining on us rapidly, there was apparently no immediate
danger. Strange to say, we had struck upon the rocks at
just about the same time in the morning that we had

collided with the iceberg—that is, at twenty minutes after eight o'clock.

At about half-past nine two little specks were discerned in the distance, alternately appearing and disappearing with the motion of the waves, and as we drew nearer these turned out to be two Eskimo pilots in kayaks. With great skill they ran alongside the ship, unhitched themselves from their gear, and came aboard. Then the governor's boat hove in sight; for our signals of distress had been heard, and it bore the crack pilot of these waters. By eleven o'clock we were safely anchored in the harbor of Sukkertoppen, and the *Miranda* was tied with cables to ring-bolts in the rocks.

Now a more careful examination as to the damage the rocks had done us was made—though, of course, it could not be fully ascertained. It was discovered, however, that whatever hole the rocks had made was just beneath the ballast-tank. This tank extended the whole width of the ship, and lay beneath the engine-room and stoke-hold. It was empty when the *Miranda* left Sukkertoppen; but on her return after the accident was found to be full of water, and the pumps could make no impression upon it. It was fortunate for us that the force of the blows had been sustained by this portion of the ship, for had the rocks gored anywhere else we should have gone to the bottom at once. The top of the ballast-tank acted as a false bottom and kept us afloat; but the top of this tank was thin and worn and coated with rust, liable to burst at any minute if subjected to a rough sea. Hence the captain at once decided that it was unsafe to venture forth in the *Miranda*, and the question of how we were to get home again stared us in the face.

Here was a pretty how-de-do. We were stranded in Greenland. Provisions already were beginning to run short, and the settlement could not afford us any, having a bare sufficiency for itself. There was no chance of getting away before spring, unless we secured some vessel cruising about in the vicinity. There was a bare chance that the *Falcon* might be intercepted on her return from Peary's headquarters; but then the *Falcon*, being a small ship, could accommodate only a few of us, at best, in addition to those she had on board. We learned from the governor that there were two or three American schooners at the fishing-banks of Holsteinborg, about a hundred and fifty miles away. Here, then, was our chance of getting back to civilization; but how one of these schooners finally came to our rescue must be told in another chapter.

CHAPTER IV.

WHEN it was ascertained that we should have to remain at Sukkertoppen until some vessel could be secured to rescue us we at once set about organizing parties for various expeditions. Of course, the most important thing was to secure one or more of the fishing-schooners reported to be off the fishing-banks near Holsteinborg, about one hundred and forty miles away. A relief party was selected to go to Holsteinborg for this purpose under the command of Dr. Cook. The other members of the party were Messrs. Ladd, Rogers, Porter, Thompson, and Dunning. Captain Farrell gave Dr. Cook the following letter, to be given to the captain of any ship that he might find:

"SUKKERTOPPEN, SOUTH GREENLAND,
"August 10, 1894.

"*To Whom It May Concern :*

"DEAR SIR:—The steamer *Miranda*, of Liverpool, England, from New York, with Dr. Frederick A. Cook's Arctic Expedition, struck a sunken rock seven miles southwest of this harbor. The ship is making water. Dr. Cook is going to you for immediate assistance, which please send, as we are in distress.

"Yours truly,
"CAPT. WM. J. FARRELL,
"Master of Steamship *Miranda*."

Governor Bistrup placed an open sailboat at the disposal

SIMILIK GLACIER.

of the party, and sent a Dane and four picked Eskimos along with it. The expedition started on the evening of August 10. On that date two other parties started out—a party to explore the Similik glacier, composed of Professors Wright and Jillson, and Messrs. Dove, F. Wright, Jr., Kersting, Orth, Rumrill, and Brown ; and a party to go up the Isortok fiord to hunt and fish, composed of Dr. Cramer, Professor Freeman, Dr. Stebbins, and Messrs. Gay, Joyner, Garrison, and myself. We took along with us Clark, one of the waiters, who proved himself an invaluable man, and five Eskimos as guides. We had two boats, which were pretty well loaded with our tents, provisions, baggage, guns, etc., to say nothing of ourselves and the guides. Our main object was to hunt deer. We went over the same course that I had previously been over in going to the glacier, except that we eventually passed the glacier and went about fifteen miles farther on.

At about eight o'clock in the evening we reached an island near the mouth of Isortok fiord, and here we pitched our tents for the night. Clark cooked us an excellent meal, though we had to be sparing with our provisions, for on the *Miranda* we had already been put on short rations of two meals per diem. At the start the stocking of the ship had been put in the hands of a steward who was entirely new to the business. He was a recent Yale graduate and an excellent linguist, but, like the famous Miss Von Blurkey,

"Both Latin and Greek he could fluently speak,
But he did not know chicken from turkey."

Had the worst come to the worst, he might perhaps have supplied us with enough Greek roots to have kept us all alive.

The next day it was raining hard, and the Eskimos, whom we had to consult in matters of this kind, declared that we could not proceed. They were very positive weather prophets, and it must be admitted that they did understand their own climate pretty well. They looked at the sky, observed the course of the winds, shook their heads, and said "No goot," "no goot," this phrase being the extent of their knowledge

SOME YOUNG PROPHETS.

of English, and then dove into a little cavern, in which they made their quarters. They had covered the mouth of this cavern with a sail. It was evidently a favorite resort for Eskimo outing parties, as it was full of fish-bones and refuse of all kinds, and had a most abominable odor; this seemed to make them feel at home and happy.

In the afternoon it lightened up a little, and Dr. Cramer and Professor Freeman decided to go back to the *Miranda* for some oilskins; at our camp we were only about twelve miles from the ship. They coaxed a couple of Eskimos from their redolent cavern and started away in our smaller boat, with the intention of coming back as soon as the storm was over. Later it began to rain in real dead earnest. That night was one of the most uncomfortable I have ever spent. Our tent had been injudiciously pitched on a side-hill, and so a small waterfall percolated through the mossy floor. Greenland moss makes an excellent bed when dry, but when it rains it quickly becomes like a wet sponge. We could make no fire, because there was nothing to burn except moss, which at the time was impossible, and the night was very cold. We had a little oil-stove, which we kept going until it burned out; but this did not help matters much. The tent's roof was so wet that great drops fell on our upturned faces as we lay huddled together in the middle of the camp, and I could push my boot down in the wet moss and hear the water gurgle. There was not much sleep that night for anybody. We fell to talking about comfortable waterproof beds in order to divert our minds. "Did you ever sleep in two empty flour barrels?" remarked Clark, whose experiences seemed to have been varied. "No,"

CARL AND HIS TWO BEST GIRLS.

said a voice; "I'll admit that I have been intoxicated, but I have never been that bad." Nevertheless, Clark went on to describe how good and dry a couch could be made of two barrels; and the idea of any kind of a dry couch was comforting.

The next day it ceased raining, except a fine drizzle; but the Eskimos still shook their heads and said "No goot." We shot some guillemots and sandpipers, which relieved the monotony of the day. In the afternoon the boat came back from the ship with the Eskimos; they brought a note from Dr. Cramer saying that all the weather prophets in Sukkertoppen predicted stormy weather for some days, and therefore he and Professor Freeman would not return until the storm was over, as it was useless to proceed until it cleared. The boat was to return to the *Miranda* that afternoon, so that any one could go back to the ship who desired to do so. I took young Carl Garrison with me and made for the *Miranda*. We needed more bread, and I wished to get a rubber blanket—a necessity for this kind of camping. It was about nine in the evening when we reached the ship. The day was Sunday, and I went over to the settlement to pay my respects to the governors and their ladies, who dwelt amicably under one roof. Here I found several of our party, for the governors' house was a very popular rendezvous, and we passed a most agreeable evening. Assistant-Governor Baumann and his wife both spoke English very well, as did also Mrs. Bistrup, who acted as interpreter for her husband. A charming young lady, Miss Fausböll, half English, half Danish, was staying

THE TWO GOVERNORS.

with Mrs. Bistrup, so altogether it was no wonder that the governors' house was extremely popular—one was sure of being most hospitably received and agreeably entertained. Mrs. Baumann sang exceedingly well, and all the ladies were well versed in English and American literature; and I must not forget to mention that the governor possessed an excellent stock of wine and cigars. The talk turned upon the Eskimos and their traits. It seemed that there had been an epidemic raging in some of the small hamlets about, which the governor attributed to the people eating putrid whale-meat—a delicate morsel among them. Six hunters from Sukkertop-

MRS. BAUMANN.   BISTRUP CHILDREN.   MRS. BISTRUP.   MISS FAUSBOLL.

pen had recently gone to an encampment where the epidemic was raging, and only two had returned; the others were stricken down. When well the natives will not listen to advice, and are very improvident; but when sick they get very much frightened. Death terrifies them exceedingly, and they mourn deeply for a few days the loss of a relative or friend; then suddenly they become merry again, and apparently think of their loss no more.

In character the Eskimo is gay and careless; if he has enough to eat he enjoys the present and gives no thought to

ENTRANCE TO AN ESKIMO HUT.

the future. He has a strongly developed sense of freedom and independence, which is natural, considering the nomad life of his ancestors. Another prominent trait is his honesty; for theft among Eskimos is very rare, and is looked upon as exceedingly reprehensible. Murder is almost unknown, and they do not make war upon one another. They are very hospitable in disposition, and are good-natured and kind-hearted. Polygamy was common before the West Coast Eskimos became converts to the Christian faith, but now monogamy is the ideal, though not always closely adhered to in practice. Occasional cases of open polygamy are still to be met with, but these are very rare. Woman, though considered inferior to man—a grading not entirely peculiar to the

Eskimo—yet enjoys a good status, and is treated with consideration. The division of labor in a household is distinct. The man is the hunter and supporter of the family; his work is performed almost exclusively upon the sea; on land he loafs and invites his soul. The women take care of the booty, skin the seals, and cut them according to prescribed rules. They prepare and cook the food, dress the skins, make clothes, cover the boats; they build and manage the houses, and even the large boats, or oomiaks. The houses are built of stone and turf, and generally contain but one room, entrance to which is effected through a long, narrow passage. In the single large room the entire family, or more often an aggregation of families, eat and sleep. There are generally several benches in this room, and upon these the inhabitants huddle together and sleep. Some of the houses have fireplaces, but mostly the room is heated by lamps burning blubber-oil. The cooking is done in a special fireplace outside, near the entry; the fuel used is peat and a kind of guano provided by the gulls. The culinary method is very simple. Meat and fish are eaten both raw and cooked, and these edibles are highly prized when in a state of decomposition, which is supposed to give a spice to them. Seal and whale blubber are eaten raw, and because the Eskimos feel the want of vegetable food they are very fond of the contents of the paunch of the reindeer—a mixture of moss and such sparse vegetation as the deer can find. A preserve made of this compound, mixed with crowberries and blubber, is another delicate morsel. "Matak," or the skin of whale or dolphin, taken off the animal with the upper layer of fat and eaten raw, is another Eskimo *bon bouche*.

The social system of the West Greenland Eskimos is a mixture of their own traditions and of modern European ways. There is a modified communism among them. They recognize private property in the kayak and its appurtenances, wearing apparel, and certain household effects. In land there is no property, and the spoils of the hunter do not belong entirely to him. In the main the whole settlement must, as far as possible, profit by the booty of a single hunter, so that families are not entirely dependent upon their own natural providers. They have laws defining the amount in regard to each animal that the hunter can keep for himself and family, and how much he must distribute among his neighbors. If

DENMARK AND GREENLAND.

the whole provision is not consumed, and there are no neighbors still in want, the hunter may put by for his winter store. But if want and famine come, then this store is brought out to be shared in common. It is a thing unknown in Greenland for some to live in abundance while others are in suffering and want about them. The Golden Rule was written upon the hearts of these people and practised long before the advent of the missionary.

Upon going back to the ship that evening I had an interesting talk with Professor Brewer, who was in charge in the absence of Dr. Cook. He had attended the Eskimo church that day, and gave me such a graphic description of the services that, with his kind permission, I subsequently made a copy of his account as given in his journal, and reproduce it herewith.

We went ashore at ten—a dozen of us. The rain had nearly ceased, and numerous rills coursed down the rocks opposite the hamlet in picturesque cascades.

THE NARROW PATH.

We had been told that the services began at ten; it was after ten, but no one had assembled, and so we waited outside.

The scene was curiously picturesque. The tide was but half in, and the little cove by the church was yet dry. On the slopes were the huts or houses of the natives, and behind the rugged rocky hills rose, their tops obscure and illy defined in the thick air. Little cascades like white ribbons hung against the sides of the gray granite hills. A few patches of snow were near—not many nor large, but enough to show what Greenland dog-days are.

With the second bell the people hurried from their houses, almost simultaneously, and the congregation was quickly assembled. We waited outside until all were in but a few stragglers, then went in, and were shown front seats, probably seats of honor; but I should have preferred to have been in the rear, where I could have seen the congregation better.

The elderly people sat in the rear and the children in front: women on the left, with the girls in front; men on the right, with most of the boys in front. There was very much coughing by the natives, especially when they came in; less so later, although there was much all through the service. The people sat very close; there were many children, and an almost continuous cooing of the babies.

The little church is of stone, the walls over three feet thick, whitewashed without, sealed with boards within; the boards painted a dull pale-blue on the sides, the ceiling white.

A raised platform extended along one end; on our right a plain desk, on the left a melodeon, or parlor organ; a reading-stand was moved to the middle by the clergyman for reading.

Back there was an altar with crucifix and two unlighted candles; in front a railing and kneeling-step, as if for communion and confirmations. The preacher was a little old man with thin face and spectacles, in blouse and hood and sealskin boots. He was probably a Dane, but so bronzed that he was as dark as many of the natives. He had a kindly face and kindly, plaintive voice, his whole look and voice in keeping with the place. The service began at 10.45 and ended at about 11.50.

After invocation and prayers, there was singing by the congregation, with the organ. There seemed to be less difference between the male and female voices than with our race. The melody was excellent, and also the time; the voices rich, but thin. The only dragging I heard was when some of our party took up the time and sang with them. The tunes were Lutheran, and had a familiar sound, as we have hymn-tunes based on them.

The hymns were long; the singing was prolonged and

AT THE CHURCH DOOR.

pleasing in the extreme. There was a charm about it that was to me simply delightful. After the singing came what I took to be a sermon, read, which lasted about twenty-five minutes; then more singing and prayers—the singing of the second time impressing me even more than the first. The time was so well kept; not a note of discord. Afterwards, short prayers, during which the babies cooed again; not one cried

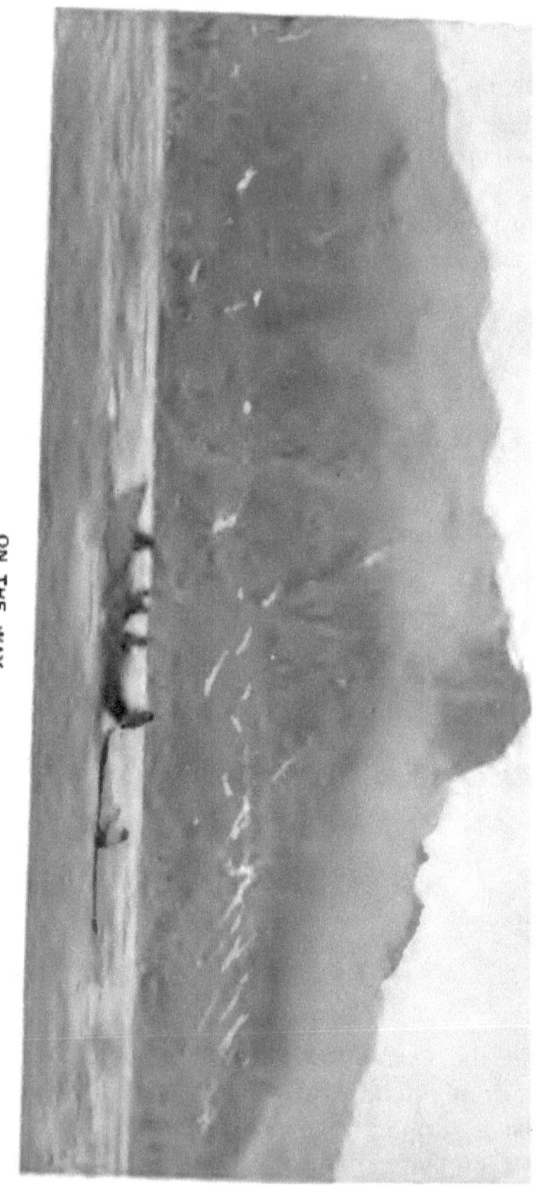

ON THE WAY.

during the service, but during the last part one or two fretted with that peculiar fret which civilized mothers recognize as a sign of hunger. I suppose the same was the case here, for I noticed that in each case it stopped suddenly, and that baby was not heard from again.

At the close the women went out first, the men remaining in their seats until all the women were out, and until we left. Indeed, I did not see them come out, as we went directly to our boat and returned to the ship.

Of the many churches and congregations I have attended services in and with, never one more interesting than this. The church, the race, the quaint costumes, the service, entirely in the Eskimo tongue, the music, the simple service and devout attention, made a picture and left a profound impression.

We were unable to make a start for the camp until August 14. It had rained hard and continually, and the sea was so high that the Eskimos would not venture forth, and the governor advised us strongly to trust to their instincts. In the afternoon of that day it stopped raining, and we finally induced the Eskimos to make a start, though they consented with evident unwillingness. We had hardly been out more than an hour when the rain began again to fall in torrents, and a high wind dead against us, and a high sea, made it the hardest kind of work to reach again the shelter of the islands in our little archipelago. For some time we seemed to be running a dead heat with a large rock not far to starboard; for an hour or so we did not gain a foot, but just managed to hold our own against wind and tide. The poor Eskimos pulled like Trojans. I had hold of the helm, and had great difficulty in keeping the boat's head to the wind and waves. My hands, incased in woollen mittens, wringing wet, were so numb that I could hardly keep hold of the tiller. We had an uncomfortable night at camp again, but not nearly so bad as

THE MORNING BREAKS.

the former one, because the morning after that memorable night we had selected a better camping-ground upon a dead level, so that although our floor was undoubtedly moist, it did not this time resemble a swamp.

When morning broke it was clear and beautiful, and we started at last for our happy hunting-grounds in most excellent spirits. The unveiling, as it were, of the magnificent scenery about us by the sun's dispersal of the heavy mists and fog was one of the grandest and most impressive sights I have ever witnessed. Most of the mountain ranges in the distance stood out distinctly in the clear sun, but the loftiest peaks were still veiled by white clouds of mist. The keen, clear air after the damp and fog was exhilarating in the extreme, and we broke out into the wildest shouts and bacchanalian songs, to the great amusement of our Eskimo friends. Just as we were starting and had our boats ready to push off, we suddenly heard a volley of shots, and a large oomiak hove in sight, containing a band of joyful Eskimos who were returning from a deer-hunt. They had captured twenty-four deer, so they indicated, and held up a number of deer-horns to prove their assertion. The body of one of their comrades who had died on the expedition was lying in the bottom of their boat, but this did not seem to interfere with their cheerfulness. Most of them landed and gazed at us with the greatest curiosity and wonder, for they had been away in camp since before our arrival. We parted with many salutations and expressions of good will conveyed through gestures.

We had a magnificent pull that day of about thirty miles up the Isortok fiord, blazing away now and then at a guillemot or a puffin. We had a kayak in tow—a most useful boat in an excursion of this kind; for whenever a bird fell one of the Eskimos would get in the kayak, go back and pick up the bird, and rejoin us without delaying our progress. After we had passed the glacier that I mentioned before, we rowed by some wonderful loomeries of seagulls. Steep, precipitous cliffs rose to a height of two or three thousand feet straight upward from the water, and these were thickly dotted with thousands upon thousands of seagulls, perched in crowds on

UP ISORTOK FIORD.

ledges everywhere. As the Eskimos are very fond of a seagull stew, and made signs that they would like to have some of the birds, we fired a few shots at some of the crowded ledges, and about half a dozen birds fell at every shot. They filled the bottom of our boat, and looked so downy white and pretty that it seemed almost a shame to sacrifice them, but our provisions were so scarce that this slaughter of the innocents was a necessity. The shots caused the birds to jump from their perches, and soon countless thousands of screaming gulls were circling all about us. It was impossible to make any adequate estimate of their numbers.

We reached our camping-grounds at about four o'clock in the afternoon, and pitched our two tents upon a mossy plateau on the banks of a narrow stream. All around us the great, gaunt mountains arose, and near by a huge glacier coursed downward to the sea. The next morning we were up by five o'clock, and each one took an Eskimo guide, and going his own way, started to hunt the reindeer which are said to inhabit these regions. By nightfall the party were back in camp again, tired, hungry, disappointed; for not a deer had even been seen. We had ascended high mountains and descended into valleys, clambered over rocks and snow, and all sorts of precipitous places, but not even the sight of a

HUNTING GROUNDS.

deer had rewarded our efforts. Here and there we found footprints, but this was all. I regret to have to record this fact; but as a truthful historian I am compelled to admit that, though we wandered over this country for days, we saw no deer at all. Either a bird had carried the news to the deer that we were coming and they had wisely moved inland, or—

a somewhat more probable supposition—the Eskimos did not want us to get any deer, and had brought us to an unlikely spot—a ground that had recently been hunted over. The reindeer are very necessary to the Eskimos, not only for food, but also for their skins, which are utilized for various purposes; small wonder, then, if they are not anxious to assist

NO DEER IN SIGHT.

strangers in capturing these valuable animals. Had we had time to strike our tents and move inland, I have no doubt we should have found fine sport. Clark, indeed, reported that he had seen deer on several occasions about the camp when the rest of us were far away; but Clark was not fond of solitude, and was apt to solace himself by fishing out of the tent some hidden bottle; and after he had indulged in a solitary *séance* he was apt to see any animal—not excepting snakes. But though we got no deer, we caught quantities of salmon and salmon-trout in the stream near us, and also lake-trout, in the clear fresh-water lakes, which were all about us. Our stream was simply teeming with fish. I know that fish stories are generally taken with a grain of salt, and often with more liberal quantities; but as I have been truthful about the deer, though in so far-away a region it would be easy to draw upon the imagination without detection, my word should be relied upon as regards the amount of fish we caught. This is a fact: during an afternoon's sport one of our party caught one hundred and sixty-two salmon-trout, and another within an hour's time captured forty-five. The Eskimos had a little set-net with which they caught some beautiful large salmon, and they also gaffed the fish with great skill. We simply revelled in salmon and trout. I know of nothing finer than a salmon just out of the water, or a large salmon-trout baked upon a flat rock. Any one who has indulged in this luxury out in the open after a day's sport can bear me out in the assertion. Up in the highlands we found those delicious birds, the ptarmigan, and on the water we shot guillemots, murres, and puffin, so that we managed to live well in spite of our lack of venison.

On August 19 we bid a regretful farewell to our camp, for it was time for us to get back to the *Miranda*. Dr. Cook was expected back within ten days from the time of starting, and we did not want to take any chances of causing a delay. We carried back to our comrades on the ship two hundred pounds of salmon. There was one thing we were glad to leave behind us, and that was an old familiar pest—the mosquito. I have come to think that Greenland is the fatherland of the mosquito; for over its wastes it breeds and multiplies in a way that gives evidence of a most conducive environ-

PROFESSOR WRIGHT'S CAMP.

ment. We made face-masks of mosquito-netting and wire to wear when out hunting, otherwise the torture would have been unbearable. All day long we rowed, spelling each other at intervals, and reached the ship at about ten in the evening. Of course, it was still light at that time. We had no night as we understand it, only a few hours of dusk or twilight. We were about forty miles from the Arctic Circle. Across that the Arctic summer is one long day.

> " A polar day, which will not see
> A sunset till its summer's gone—
> Its sleepless summer of long light,
> The snow-clad offspring of the sun."

The glacier party had returned a few hours earlier, but Dr. Cook and his associates had not yet put in an appearance. Professor Wright and his party were much pleased with the results of their trip, although they, as we, had had a pretty rough time of it with rain and wind storms. They had been enabled during the few fine days to explore and measure several glaciers pretty thoroughly, however, and Mr. Kersting had secured a number of photographs—pictures taken with great labor and pains, and destined soon to be carried down into the sea. From notes supplied by him I am enabled to give a brief account of this expedition. The party started August 9 in a whale-boat, loaned by Governor Bistrup, with two dories from the *Miranda* as convoys. They took with them five Eskimos as guides and to help with the rowing. At sunset they reached Ikamuit, a small Eskimo settlement containing four houses. The year before the place had been almost entirely swept away by a great body of water that rushed down from a neighboring mountain and swept away the little igloos and drowned several inhabitants. Ikamuit signifies " place without shelter." The party found it worthy of its name, for they were caught in the same storm that overtook

ALONG SIMILIK FIORD.

our hunting-party, and had much the same kind of an experience. For six days they were pinned to their camp by the fury of the elements, and only short excursions were taken in the immediate neighborhood. On Sunday, the third day out, the storm abated somewhat, and in rambling in the vicinity of the camp Mr. Kersting came across an Eskimo girl engaged in pulling the skins from a number of ducks that had evidently been killed several days, for the flesh was black and covered with maggots. She scraped these from one of the ducks, and offered it to the stranger with true Eskimo hospitality. But he refused the generous offer: so she laughingly took her ducks where they would be appreciated, and soon the entire little settlement fell upon the birds and devoured them, without either cooking or cleaning. *De gustibus non est disputandum.*

In front of the camp ran a little brook, and here the party performed their ablutions, and here the Eskimos would gather to watch them go through these strange and novel performances. The process of brushing the teeth filled them with unbounded wonder, but when one of the party removed a set of artificial teeth and washed them there was almost a terrified stampede, and he became an object of superstitious awe and veneration. Surely a man who could remove his teeth could remove mountains.

On Sunday morning a simple service was held by the natives in one of the huts; it consisted mostly of the singing of hymns. In the afternoon Professor Wright held service in the tent, and all the Eskimos attended.

On the following day members of the party tried their hands at fishing, but did not have much success until a couple of little Eskimo girls came along and set the pace for them. They carried a short stick with a sealskin line attached about five feet in length. They threw these lines by the rocks and pulled them up and down, and soon had a mess of cod. The

Eskimo method was adopted with success by the stranger-fishermen. Quantities of black mussels were found, which were converted into an excellent soup.

On the 14th a dory containing Messrs. Dove and Rumrill started for the *Miranda*. Mr. Dove was wearied of Greenland camp-life, and Mr. Rumrill returned to get some oil and other necessary articles. On Thursday the weather cleared, tents were struck, and all hands took to the boats and pulled away to make the Similik glacier. On several occasions the camp had been left entirely in charge of the Eskimos, and though it contained for them great luxuries, such as coffee and tobacco, nothing was touched or taken. On Friday the party clambered over the great glacier and made about five miles toward the inland ice, crossing broad crevasses, and carefully avoiding many pitfalls, cracks, and soft snow.

On Saturday the party started for Sukkertoppen, but had not proceeded far before they were overtaken by a severe storm and were forced to take shelter upon an island. They managed to get up a tent, but so strong was the wind that members of the party spelled one another all night long in holding the tent down and keeping it and their belongings from being blown into the water. On the next day the party succeeded in getting back to the *Miranda*, tired out with their fierce struggle with the elements, but happy over the ultimate success of their trip. The results of this trip, as well as other observations on glacial phenomena, are given by Professor Wright in the able article which he has contributed to this book.

At about nine o'clock on the morning of August 20 a great cheer arose, and on going on deck I saw a small schooner riding in to our harbor, surrounded by great numbers of kayaks. It was not long before Dr. Cook and his party came rowing over to the *Miranda*, and they were received with great enthusiasm, as can well be imagined. The schooner they had secured was the *Rigel*, commanded by Captain George W. Dixon, of Gloucester, Mass. The history of the expedition after the schooner is a very interesting one, and I have abridged it from the diary of one of the members, Mr. Russell W. Porter, who kindly placed his notes at my disposal. For a fuller description of this trip I can refer my readers to Mr. Porter's own narrative.

The expedition started, as I mentioned before, at about six o'clock on the evening of August 10. Early the next morning they arrived at Kangarmuit, otherwise known as Old Sukkertoppen. Here they remained for a day and a half on account of bad weather, being allowed by the governor to take up their quarters in the loft of the church, as there was no other building large enough to accommodate the party. On Sunday morning, the 12th, they started away, and sailed until eleven that night, when they camped upon a small island. They broke camp the following morning, but as there was a heavy wind and rain storm, they found that they could make no progress, and were obliged to go into camp again. For two days the storm continued, and they had great difficulty in keeping the tent from blowing away. The party finally got away early on August 15, and sailed and rowed for sixteen hours, arriving at Holsteinborg at eight o'clock in the evening. On the way they stopped at Itirdlek, a small settlement, to inquire about the schooners. No schooners were there, but some were reported at Nepisat, not far away; they went to Nepisat, but found no ships, and so went on to Holsteinborg. As they neared this place they ran up the American flag and fired a salute with rifles; a Danish flag was immediately run up on shore, and an answering salute fired from the governor's cannon. They were hospitably entertained by Governor Müller, of Holsteinborg, who made the party take their meals at his house, and gave them a room in one of his outhouses. They found out that the schooner *Rigel*, of

TERMINAL MORAINE.

Gloucester, Mass., had left Holsteinborg on the previous day for the Banks, and that there were five other schooners outside. Three of the party were detailed to go to the top of a neighboring mountain, eighteen hundred feet high, to look for a schooner with a spy-glass; but they had hardly started before a schooner was seen bearing west by south. Mr. Rogers went back to inform Dr. Cook, and an Eskimo in a kayak was sent over to the schooner. Two of the party continued the ascent of the mountain, and plunged into a driving snow-storm about four hundred feet from the summit. In the evening they returned to the governor's house, where the party was assembled, and shortly afterward news was brought that a dory had been sighted coming up the harbor. The dory proved to contain Captain Dixon, of the schooner *Rigel*. The schooner had been five months out from Gloucester, and had recently come from fishing on the Iceland coast.

The day before several couriers had been despatched in kayaks to scour the surrounding waters for any of the reported schooners, and they bore letters from Dr. Cook calling for assistance. One of these couriers had boarded the *Rigel* near Itirdlet, and so Captain Dixon had come over post-haste to Holsteinborg, arriving at about ten o'clock in the evening. In talking over the matter with Dr. Cook Captain Dixon said that before he could go to the rescue of the people on board the *Miranda* he would have to consult with his crew, as they were co-operative sharers in the profits of the fishing trip, which would have to be abandoned if the rescue were made at once. He said that his trip would be over about September 5, and that he could then call at Sukkertoppen; but if his men were willing to give up the trip and start for Sukkertoppen at once he would bring his schooner up in the offing in the morning and fly his flag as a signal. He then left to go back to the *Rigel*.

The following morning a man was detailed to mount the

hill and look for a signal from the schooner. She was sighted flying her flag and making north. The party collected their baggage, and after bidding farewell to the hospitable governor they boarded the *Rigel*, which was lying about a mile from the harbor, and set sail for Sukkertoppen. Captain Dixon was obliged to exercise much caution, for the waters

THE COMING OF THE RIGEL.

were strange to him, and three dangers threatened him—fog, ice, and sunken rocks. As it was, the schooner struck a sunken rock at the outset of the journey, but after bumping several times she cleared it without serious damage.

On the morning of August 20, when the schooner had been sighted from the *Miranda*, Captain Farrell rowed out to meet her, and it was not long before the two captains had

come to terms. It was agreed between them that $4,000
should be paid to Captain Dixon as a recompense for breaking
in upon his fishing trip, and for carrying the passengers to
some port where they could get transportation home. It was
also agreed that the schooner should accompany the *Miranda*
to some convenient port of repair, and that the crew of the
schooner should hold themselves in readiness to rescue the
officers and crew of the *Miranda* in case the steamer should
founder or have to be abandoned—the recompense for this to
be settled by arbitration, or by mutual agreement between the
agents of the schooner and the underwriters of the *Miranda*.

At first glance it might seem to the reader that $4,000 for
taking the party to a port of safety was rather high; but a few
words suffice to show that it was only a just and moderate
charge. In the first place, it must be remembered that our
party, with the *Miranda's* crew, numbered seventy-five men
all told, making the price per head a trifle over fifty-three
dollars. Then Captain Dixon was obliged to give up finishing out his fishing trip, and a trip into these regions means
considerable expense and great hardships. An average catch
of halibut would net $6,000. Again, half the sum netted by
a fishing schooner of the kind goes to the owners of the
vessel; the remainder is divided between the captain and
crew. Indeed, Captain Dixon generously offered to take the
entire party homeward for nothing if they would consent to
remain in Greenland two or three weeks longer and allow him
to finish his fishing. But the inadequate stock of provisions
made it dangerous to remain even for this short period of
time. In truth, the expedition was at the mercy of this big-
hearted captain; he could have demanded any sum that he
pleased. As it turned out, the contract made proved to be
in no way binding upon the *Miranda's* owners. They felt
themselves in nowise bound to pay the $4,000, and did not
do so. They held that in losing the ship, notwithstanding

its insurance, they had themselves suffered considerable loss. The law does not hold a company responsible for a contract made with a captain under these circumstances. Had the *Miranda* been brought into port, then Captain Dixon would have had a legally recognized claim. As it was, he could not recover even for the losses he had sustained in making room for the passengers and crew of the steamer. At no time, before or after the repudiation of the contract, has Captain Dixon made any claim upon the passengers of the *Miranda* for the great service he had rendered them. Of their own volition they started a subscription, to which the *Miranda's* company contributed two hundred and fifty dollars, and have forwarded him something over one-half the sum the contract called for. This little volume has been issued in the hope that the profits arising from its sale may at least amount to a fair portion of the balance morally, if not legally, due to the captain and crew of the *Rigel*.

After the agreements between the two captains had been drawn up and witnessed by the first officer of the *Miranda* and the two Governors of Sukkertoppen, preparations were immediately made for the reception of the *Miranda's* passengers on board the *Rigel*. There were four bunks in the after-cabin, which were reserved for the older members of our party. A place was cleared in the after-hold, used mainly as a store-room for salt ; fifty hundredweight of salt was taken out, with some lumber, and presented to the Eskimos, and $800 worth of fishing tackle was thrown away, in order to make room for our party. Thus a space was cleared about twenty feet long, fifteen wide, and four feet high ; a door communicated with the cabin, and in this space sleeping room for thirty passengers was divided off. The crew of the *Rigel* willingly turned out of their quarters to make room for the *Miranda's* passengers, and all crowded into the forecastle.

The evening of August 20 was our last at Sukkertoppen.

Most of our party went over to pay their final respects to the kind governors and their ladies, for it was arranged that we should start on the following morning. As I came out of the governors' house I found an Eskimo dance in progress on a little square near the house. Two or three Eskimo girls at once seized me and laughingly pulled me into the dance—a very lively and energetic one—and so I jigged away for an

COMING TO SAY GOOD-BYE.

hour or more, to my own amusement and that of the Eskimos. And how they do dance, these little people! With their whole bodies and with their whole souls. An Eskimo dance is a scene of life, of rapid movement, of intense enjoyment. No sad funereal faces, or bodies somberly clad in black, as if in deep mourning for their folly or their sins, and moving dejectedly and regretfully, among the jovial Eskimo men. And the women, their lithe bodies clad in garments that give freedom to every movement; they do not appear to think that there is any credit in being jolly at a dance. How they fling and swing themselves about, dancing in perfect time—dancing all over, from the tip-top of their waving, nodding top-knots to the tips of their energetic little toes! I should like to witness with what wonder, with what laughter, these little ladies would

A FAREWELL GLIMPSE.

look upon the sad-eyed swains at one of our fashionable balls. They make the best of their surroundings, despite their hard environment. Verily, verily, an Eskimo missionary might teach us a few things.

The Eskimo dances are not national. European and American whalers have been the dancing-masters, and so the Eskimos can waltz and polka, but the reel they love best, and a variety of reels they have made their own, and these have assumed a certain national character.

It was cold and misty the next morning, and a fine drizzle was falling. Canvas had been spread over the salt in the after-hold of the schooner, and over this we put our mattresses side by side. Each man had just his mattress room,—that was all,—and every bit of space was taken up. On account of the limited space, we could bring only a few necessaries on the schooner. The little vessel was but ninety-nine feet long, and of one hundred and seven tons burden.

GOVERNORS' HOUSE.

To insure against separation in case of fog or in the darkness, it was decided that the steamer should tow the schooner, so the two were connected with a cable line, and a system of signals was arranged between the two captains, in order that they could communicate in case of need or accident. It was hoped that the *Miranda* could make the run to St. Johns with safety, or at any rate that she could be run in somewhere on the Labrador coast. At about ten o'clock we got under way. The American flag was run up on our mainmast, and was greeted with loud cheers. The *Miranda* being an English ship, and sailing under a British charter, of course, flew English colors, so now for the first time we were sailing under the Stars and Stripes. We all removed our hats, though a drizzling rain was falling, and sang in a swelling chorus the "Star-Spangled Banner," and "My Country, 'tis of Thee."

It was an impressive scene, and one that will always live in my memory. Near us, in a large boat, rowed by Eskimos, were the governors and their ladies, who had come to bid us a final farewell. We gave them cheer upon cheer, which they returned, and in which the Eskimo rowers joined. On shore a solid phalanx of Eskimos was drawn up, rapidly firing parting salutes, and all about us the kayaks darted, and the little kayakers waved us a last good-by. Gradually the *Miranda* towed us out of the harbor into the open sea, and the mists fell about us, and the shores of Greenland were hidden from our sight. And another mist, too, gathered in the eyes of many a member of the expedition, straining his vision to catch a last glimpse of a place that had become endeared to us all by many acts of courtesy and kindness. There is a deep pathos in a farewell when human beings whom chance has brought together in the close companionship of strange places look upon one another's faces for the last time, knowing that in life they shall not meet again. Farewell—a long farewell to the warm hearts in that stout little Danish house perched on the cold and barren rocks of Greenland; and farewell, too, to the little people who gather near by and make the night merry with dancing and laughter! Somewhere—somewhere, when the mists have all rolled away, may we meet again!

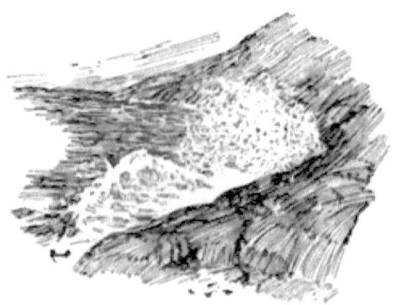

CHAPTER V.

The rain which began to fall on the morning we started from Sukkertoppen continued to fall for four days with scarcely an intermission. There was no shelter to seek on deck of any kind; it was cold, wet, and disagreeable, while below the air was so close and foul that it made most of us seasick, so that we alternated between the devil and the deep sea with a vengeance. A generous mixture of the odor of fish and bilge-water in an overcrowded apartment in the after-hold combined to make the most powerful and, I think, the most disagreeable smell that I have ever been subjected to. To add to our misery, the hatchway, which supplied light and air to the after-hold, had often to be closed on account of the stormy weather, as for a great part of the time the waves were washing all over our decks. In the night the extremely close quarters, the foul odor, and the groans, to say nothing of other noises, of the seasick ones, made us feel as if we had descended into a veritable miniature inferno. But perpetual adaptation to environment, says Spencer, is the law of life; and, in accordance with this kindly law, we gradually grew accustomed to our new surroundings, and our sense of smell grew dull even to bilge-water.

Owing to the size of the schooner's cooking-stove, it was impossible to prepare for so large a crowd more than two meals a day, and these meals were necessarily limited to a

CAPTAIN GEORGE W. DIXON.

few articles of consumption. Salt beef, fish chowder, halibut
fins, potatoes, oatmeal, coffee, tea, and bread were the staple
articles of food and drink. We did not enjoy all these deli-
cacies at any one time, of course, for the cook varied them
with excellent judgment. The cook, too, had a fine and epi-
curean imagination, which helped us out not a little. For if,
like the Marchioness with her orange-peel and water, we all
made believe a good deal, and tried to live up to the cook's
romantic descriptions of his viands, we fared very sumptu-
ously indeed. As he ladled out the solitary viand or two upon
the tin plates which served as an *omnium gatherum* and
passed them to a waiter standing at the entrance to his little
cock-pit, his cheery voice would ring out: "Pass round
the roast goose,
George; apple
sass, and a little
paddy de foi grass,
turkey, or chicken
fricasee, if the
gents prefer it!
Fill the glasses
with claret, then
pass round the
champagne—live-
ly, George — live-
ly!" etc. While
to offset this ro-
manticism the
realistic George
would shout in
stentorian tones: "One on the salt horse, without harness!
One on halibut fin!" However, I noted comrades who were
epicures on shore picking at halibut fin with rare relish, for
there is no sauce like hunger; and then, as the Marchioness

THE GOOD SHIP RIGEL.

said, if you only make believe enough, orange-peel and water is very nice indeed.

As only about fifteen of us could get into the little forecastle, which served both as a general dining-room and a sleeping-room for the *Rigel's* crew, we managed to keep the cook pretty busy; in fact, the meals lasted the greater part of the day. The forecastle was small, but it afforded a great variety of motion; for here the pitching and tossing of the little vessel could be felt in full force. It was like being tossed in a blanket almost, for at times a powerful jerk would come from the *Miranda* along the tow-line that would seem to send the little schooner flying in the air. But it was not long before the steamer and the schooner were obliged to part company—a thing which, judging from the strain on the cable, they were perpetually endeavoring to accomplish.

On the second day out—August 23—we encountered very heavy swells, and we could see that the *Miranda* was rolling badly. How long the top of the ballast-tank could stand the strain of so heavy a sea was a question that was answered sooner than we anticipated. As darkness fell about us a red light gleamed from the steamer's deck, indicating that trouble was anticipated. At a few minutes after midnight three shrieks came from the steamer's whistle in rapid succession. This was the signal that she was in sore distress, and the red light was hung over the stern as a warning for Captain Dixon to be in readiness. The speed of the *Miranda* was slackened, and as the two vessels came together Captain Farrell hailed Captain Dixon to be ready, as the steamer was in a sinking condition. Immediately Captain Dixon hailed back to him to cut the cable and drop off in the boats, and that the *Rigel* would pick them up. But Captain Farrell answered back that he would try to stand by the ship until daylight. Captain Dixon hailed again, begging Captain Farrell to take no risks. The gains that salvage would bring him appeared not to influence him in the least; his only thought was for the safety of his fellow-men upon the doomed ship, and his great human heart beat in anxiety for them.

Shortly after eleven o'clock at night a fire had broken out

THE SECOND DAY OUT.

in the second cabin of the *Miranda*, and this had hardly been extinguished when the chief engineer, Mr. Dibbs, reported that the top of the water-ballast tank had given way under the immense strain caused by the high sea. At the sight of water rushing in the firemen stampeded to the deck in a panic, and attempted to launch one of the lifeboats, but only succeeded in smashing it against the iron sides of the ship. Captain Farrell promptly restored order, and the firemen were sent below again. The leaks in the tank were partially stopped by means of pillows and mattresses stuffed into the holes; but this was only a temporary expedient: the ship was in a sinking condition, and the signals of distress were given.

From the deck of the *Rigel* we could dimly see preparations going on aboard the *Miranda* for leaving the ship, though sometimes we lost sight of her altogether in the hollow of the sea. At the capstan of the schooner stood Captain Dixon with a sharp axe in hand, ready to cut the hawser that connected us with the *Miranda* should she suddenly founder and sink. It was an anxious time for us on the schooner, straining our eyes in the darkness upon the flaring red light of the *Miranda*, ever appearing and disappearing as the ship rolled in the heavy sea.

As the gray dawn began to streak the sky the first boat-load of the *Miranda's* crew came rowing over to the *Rigel*. This contained the steward and several of his men, and as soon as they were safe on board the boat was sent over to the *Miranda* again, and three dories from the *Rigel* were also launched. It was a sight long to be remembered, that of the little boats plying between the disabled steamer and the schooner, and bringing over the crew in sections, and such necessary baggage as could hastily be got together. The boats rose and fell on the swelling sea, and were often lost to view, only to rise again on the crest of some huge wave. Wonderfully well managed were these little boats by some of the gallant, stout-hearted sailors of the *Rigel*. No thought of the prize now slipping away from their grasp appeared to influence them, but with hearty good-will they bent to the oars, and carried their burdens of human freight, while all unnecessary baggage they cast into the sea. For space was very valuable upon the little schooner *Rigel*. Shortly after five o'clock in the morning the last boat-load, carrying Captain Farrell among others, arrived safely on board the schooner. The hawser had been cast off from the *Miranda*, and she was abandoned to her fate. Her lights

THE ABANDONMENT OF THE MIRANDA.

FROM A SKETCH BY A. P. ROGERS.

were still burning, her rudder had been lashed to one side, and so, with steam on and her propeller going, she slowly steamed away; and the fog fell around her like a curtain, and she was lost to sight for ever.

She might keep afloat for a few hours, but, according to the chief engineer, she was a doomed ship. Soon such temporary repairs to stop leakage as had been made would give way and the waters would close above her, and she with her precious freight would join the mighty procession of wrecks far down in the deep waters. The *Miranda* was abandoned in latitude 61° 15', longitude 58° 40', 296 miles from Sukkertoppen.

With the ship the members of the expedition lost all their belongings except the few necessaries they had brought with them on the schooner. Valuable ethnological and botanical collections (over five thousand Arctic plants had been gathered), a great number of guns and scientific instruments, the largest collection ever made of photographs of Arctic scenes and people, and quantities of stuffed birds, seals, skins, etc., all went down with the ill-fated ship. However, the saving of our own skins was matter for rejoicing, and the losses were cheerfully accepted by all hands. If the Lord loves a cheerful giver, I hope a cheerful loser may also find favor. There arose none of those bemoanings over spilled milk that are often harder to put up with than the losses themselves.

There were now ninety-three souls on board our little schooner. No time could be lost, and soon Captain Dixon was sailing with all possible speed for Hamilton Inlet, on the coast of Labrador, about 380 miles away. But fogs, head-winds, high seas, and icebergs combined to render the journey dangerous and slow as well as uncertain. It was decided to put in at the first feasible point on the Labrador coast, then pass through the straits of Belle Isle, and finally to land at Sydney, Cape Breton.

Provisions were getting very low, and it was discovered that a portion of the crew of the *Miranda* who had been lodged in the provision-hold had been systematically stealing everything edible that they could lay their hands upon, and as a consequence the larder stood in sad need of replenishment.

On August 25 the sun broke from the heavy clouds; we bathed in the sunshine for the first time since our start, and the spirits of all rose accordingly. For two evenings we had magnificent exhibitions of northern lights, and as the clearer atmosphere revealed to us numbers of white gleaming icebergs, we realized the dangers we had been passing through. On the morning of the 28th we sighted the coast of Labrador, and as the weather was threatening it was decided to make a harbor for the night. In the evening we entered Punch Bowl harbor, about sixty miles south of Rigolette. Punch Bowl is a little fishing settlement much resembling Cape Charles. Two fishing schooners were lying at anchor in this harbor: their occupants, as well as the natives of the place, gazed with wonder at the swarms of men crowding the decks of our little vessel; and the banners of the Cleveland Yacht Club and of Harvard and Yale, which we were flying, seemed also to puzzle them not a little. When, however, they learned that we were a shipwrecked party, they did not seem to evince much wonder or curiosity. Shipwrecks are a matter of such common occurrence in these regions. The most important character at Punch Bowl was a certain hard-featured old man, who was called King Bryan. He controlled the fisheries and owned the only store, so that he was monarch indeed of all he surveyed, and ruled the place—so we were given to understand—with a rod of iron. We laid in a supply of fresh codfish here, and left behind us five of the *Miranda's* crew, who were to wait for a mail steamer to take them to St. Johns, Newfoundland. They were our chief officer,

Mr. Manuel; ice-pilot Dumphy, steward Farrell, and two firemen.

In the morning, as there was no breeze, three of the dories, manned by members of the *Rigel* crew, were sent ahead, and towed us out from the sheltering harbor until we caught a breeze from the open sea. Again the dense fog fell about us, through which, every now and then, the huge dim forms of icebergs could be discerned. That night of August 30 was an anxious one for all, but especially so for Captain Dixon. In the heavy fog we sometimes passed so close to icebergs that we almost grazed them, and occasionally we could hear sounds like a cannonade as great pieces of ice broke from the bergs and fell into the

TOWING THE RIGEL.

water. The next morning the fog scaled, and by noon we had put into Henley harbor, within the straits of Belle Isle, to wait for clearer skies and a more favorable wind ; also to procure a further supply of provisions. In appearance, Henley harbor was much like the other Labrador settlements at which we had stopped, save for an enormous rock which

DEVIL'S DINING TABLE

rose up from the vicinity of the village, and which looked like a huge fort. It was flat at the top, and commanded a fine view of the harbor and of the surrounding country; the rock is called the Devil's Dining Table, though where it got this curious name I was unable to ascertain.

We remained at Henley harbor for two days; it rained most of the time, and the fog was continual. On our second and last evening I learned that a dance was in progress on shore ; and so, with two or three companions, I rowed over to attend it, having been instructed as to the whereabouts of the house of entertainment by one of the sailors. It was a dark, foggy night, and a fine, misty rain was falling. We clambered up one of the little wharves, slippery and slimy with fish, and then through a storehouse out into the open. It is no easy matter to maintain one's footing in going over these slippery wharves, and over the still more slippery floor of the storehouses; even the rocks about are slimy with fish-oil. "O'er crag and fen" we went without so much as a kindly light to guide us; at length, after scrambling over numerous large rocks, and picking our way as best we might over a bog, we ascended a steep side-hill and looked about. It is difficult to follow any given direction on a foggy night in Labrador, and as we peered about us we could discern the lights of two or three houses or huts gleaming out in the fog and darkness; but as the few houses of the settlement were scattered over a large area, we paused, not knowing which light to follow. Suddenly a moving light gleamed below us; it was a fisher-lass with a lantern, and I hailed her, but she would not answer, being evidently frightened; for she quickened her pace, and was soon enveloped in the fog. Then a dog—evidently

HENLEY HARBOR.

a large one, from his growls—made advances, and I picked up a large stone, and held a bit of hard-tack in my other hand, ready to make friend or foe, as the case might be; but after considerable snarling the dog seemed to think better of us, and retired. All of a sudden there arose a sound like the stampede of a herd of frightened cattle, and as it proceeded from a house in the dim distance, we knew that here must be the dance, and so made for it. After scaling rocks and crawling up and down wet and mossy side-hills, we at length found ourselves directly under the house, which was built on piles, and by crawling through a hole in the floor we made our entrance into one corner of the ball-room. This novel mode of entering did not appear to occasion any surprise, and indeed we were lucky to enter thus unharmed among the agile and vigorous dancers; for the floor creaked and groaned, and the entire house appeared to rock and sway, with the surprising vigor of the dance. The men wore heavy-soled boots, and every now and then as they jigged about they would whirl their fair partners fairly off their feet. It was a native Labrador dance—a combination of a round and square dance—and the most uproarious and deafening, in its effects upon the hearing, of any that I have ever attended, though we had some lively dances among the Eskimos. The orchestra was composed of a fiddler and a performer on a mouth-organ who blew loudly, fiercely, and somewhat independently of his coadjutor. The room was bare of any furniture, and a few lanterns hung from the ceiling; there were only three or four of the fair sex present, and these, of course, were in great demand. The room was mainly filled with sailors, fishermen, and tobacco smoke—a very motley group indeed; but as neither dance nor music varied much, we soon grew tired and made our way back to the schooner.

Next morning, September 2, the breeze was fair—at last—and we got off at about six o'clock. Shortly after our start we counted about twenty icebergs within sight. All day long the breeze freshened, until by night we had a regular gale, and for several hours we were obliged to lay to under a triple-reefed forsesail and forestay sail. The hatchways had to be closed; and, to add to our discomfort, the stove in the little cabin just in front of our sleeping-apartment in the salt store-room began to pour out volumes of smoke that almost choked us. One wise individual suggested that salt be thrown on the fire to put it out; the suggestion was acted upon, and immediately several shovelfuls of salt were thrust into the stove; then there issued forth clouds of smoke ten times more

HOMEWARD BOUND.

deadly and terrible than before, and as every one gasped for breath many were the invectives hurled at the head of the unfortunate man who had suggested this method of putting out a fire. Had he been turned, like Lot's wife, into a pillar of salt, I think we should have all rejoiced. However, gradually the nuisance abated, and although the odor abided with us all night and fought with the fish and bilge-water for supremacy, yet, being hardened sinners, we were enabled to snatch some sleep despite the gale and the closeness of our quarters. A small party near me, huddled together in sitting postures, kept me awake for a while by an earnest discussion of the effect of salt upon fire, as if it had not been sufficiently demonstrated. One man in particular advanced his arguments in an almost continuous stream. His extraordinary volubility had a certain fascination about it, and I could not choose but hear. At length, in a dreamy state, I gave myself up to the purely sensuous enjoyment of watching his jaws wag, and so fell asleep.

The next day the storm abated, and on this day and the next we passed a number of small fishing schooners, many of them within hailing distance. The first question invariably was: "Who have you got aboard?" and the next, "How many fish have you?" We were nearing Sydney, and the news of the wreck of the *Miranda* had evidently reached there. We were cheered here and there by a passing schooner on our identity becoming known, and on the morning of September 5 we entered, at last, with all our colors flying, the harbor of Sydney, after a remarkable voyage of fifteen days.

The story of our journey from Sukkertoppen to Sydney is so well told in Captain Dixon's log, which immediately follows this narrative, that I have purposely left out many particulars, in order to avoid vain repetitions. The familiar fog was still with us when we again dropped anchor in the harbor of Sydney, and a drizzling rain was falling; but this could not dampen our enthusiasm. It was a wild-looking party that rushed on North Sydney's shore that day, yet a most hilarious and joyous one. A bee-line was made for the post-office and cable station, and many were the messages sent to anxious ones at home telling of our safe arrival. A dinner for all hands had been arranged for at the Sydney Hotel, in Sydney proper, in the evening, and a committee was despatched to confer with

Colonel Granger and have everything in readiness. A motley crowd we were as we started for Sydney in two small steamers. The rain was falling heavily by this time, and many of the party were decked out in yellow oilskins which had seen much service, so that from a distance they looked not unlike a flock of dirty canary-birds. Then there were others arrayed in a variety of weather-beaten garments that had not been changed or taken off since the *Miranda* had faded into the mist. Many of the party carried

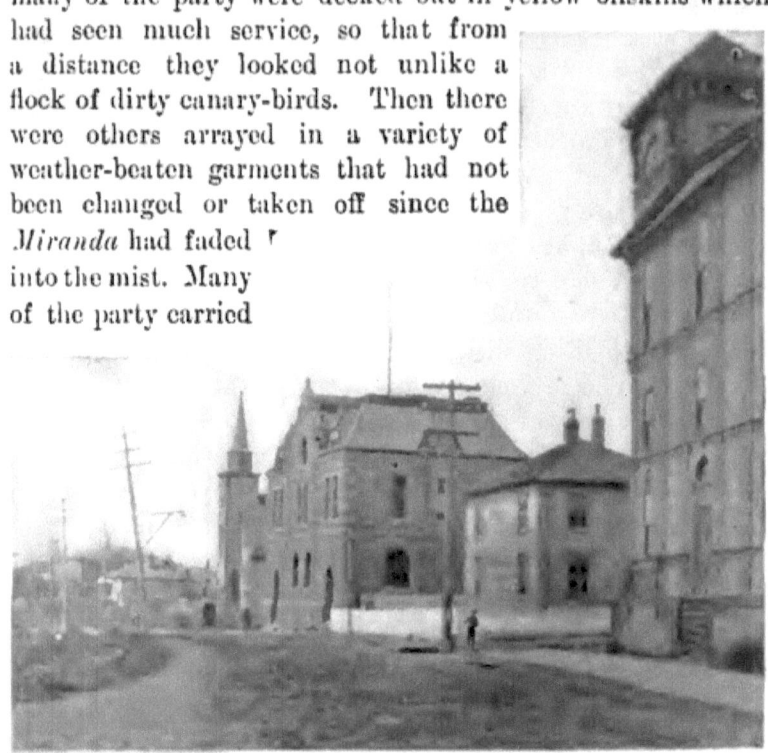

SYDNEY POST-OFFICE.

all their worldly possessions done up in gunny sacks. The parade along the streets of Sydney up to the hotel, about four blocks from the wharf, was a joyous and picturesque one. No tougher-looking gang of men ever marched over that quiet thoroughfare. One party of college students marched in a solid phalanx, chanting an original adaptation of the familiar "Hark, hark, the dogs do bark," etc., in this wise:

"Hark, hark! the dogs do bark,
The wild men are coming to town—
Some in rags, and some with jags,
And some with eider-down."

For a few eider-down quilts had been saved from the spoils.

The dinner at the Sydney Hotel was indeed "a happy time," as Captain Dixon remarks in his log. The two captains, Dixon and Farrell, were the heroes of the occasion; and the excellent repast, gotten up under the special supervision of the genial presiding genius of the hotel, Colonel

SYDNEY HOTEL—MORNING AFTER THE DINNER.

Granger, was to us, after our limited meals on the schooner, a veritable feast of the gods. The dining-hall was draped with American and English flags, and with the flags of the Cleveland Yacht Club and of Harvard and Yale—the banners that we had borne through mist and snow and ice. It was a gala night, and many were the speeches, songs, and toasts that were called out by the toast-master, Mr. James D. Dewell, of New Haven, who presided in a most happy manner. The banquet broke up at about midnight, and then farewells began to be said, for many of the party took early trains and scattered in various directions.

A large remnant of the party, however, waited to take the little steamer *St. Pierre*, which, through the courtesy of Bowring & Archibald, owners of the late *Miranda*, was sent to Sydney to take the party to Halifax, there to meet the steamer *Portia*, a sister ship of the *Miranda*, and thence to go on to New York.

With three cheers for our host, Colonel Granger, we left the comfortable Sydney Hotel and boarded the *St. Pierre*, the following morning. A snug, nice little ship she was, and we enjoyed immensely the trip to Halifax. We landed at this city on the afternoon of September 7, and found the *Portia* waiting for us, and immediately boarded her and were assigned staterooms. The *Portia*, however, was not to start for New York until ten o'clock the following morning, so we put in the time very agreeably in seeing the sights and surroundings of the beautiful city of Halifax. Here we procured New York and Boston papers several days old, which stated that the *Miranda* and its passengers and crew were probably lost; but we knew that by this time our despatches from Sydney must have been published, and that our relatives and friends were assured of our safety. It was like reading one's own obituary notice to glance over the sensational prognostications of our probable doom.

Promptly at ten o'clock on the morning of September 8 we started for New York, feeling that our adventures and dangers were a thing of the past; and yet on this short and generally uneventful trip occurred the real tragedy of our remarkable summer's outing. We started with bright and clear skies overhead; but it was not long before the long-familiar fog that had dogged us everywhere overtook us here. On the evening of the 9th a heavy fog descended and hung about us, now scaling, now falling again, and continued on the following day. We were in familiar waters off Cuttyhunk Light, and were assembled at the lunch-table at about one o'clock on the 10th. The curtain of fog had descended again; suddenly we heard the signal for reversing the engine, and the next moment we crashed into some heavy object, followed immediately by a noise as if the ship were crunching and tearing its way through some obstruction; then the *Portia* stood still and trembled. It was not such a crash as when we struck the iceberg; nor, again, such a one as we had experienced when upon the rocks off Sukkertoppen, but it was ominous enough to presage danger.

The lunch-table was quickly deserted, and on deck a scene of pitiful disaster revealed itself. We had run into a schooner and literally cut her in two, and a portion of her bow, with foremast and rigging, was lying across our deck. The fog had lifted as if by magic; for a moment we could see the stern of the schooner lifted high in air, and upon its taffrail were two men cutting away at the yawl; then the remnant of the schooner plunged into the sea and sank instantly. No other men were seen, and the rest of the crew must have been knocked overboard or sunk with the bow. As the vessel sank but one man came to the surface, afterward found to be the mate. He swam among the *débris*, and, finally reaching a spar, managed to keep afloat until rescued by a boat from the *Portia*. The other man whom we saw seemed unable to keep his head above water, but we could see him striking out under water, as if endeavoring to reach the surface; the suction was evidently too strong for him, and before our eyes he was dragged down into the sea and lost to sight. The mate,

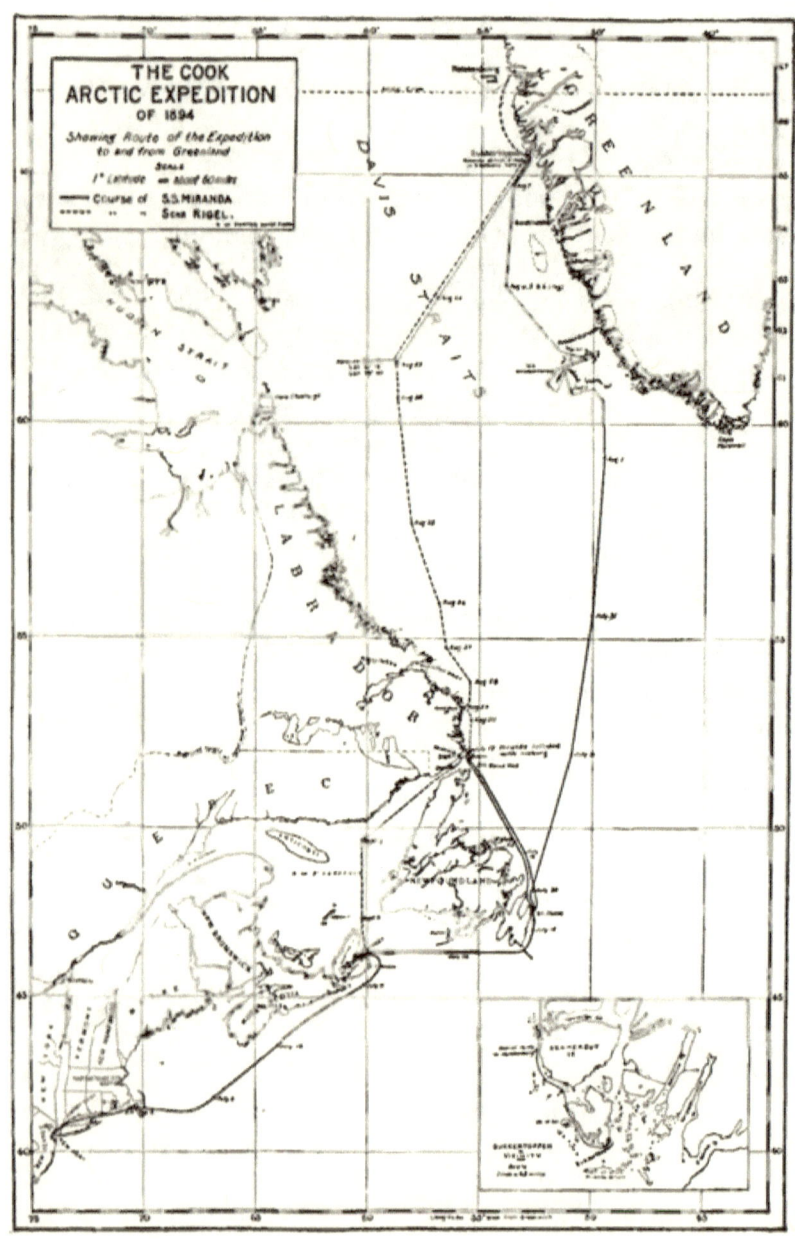

when brought aboard, was almost exhausted with his efforts, and was badly bruised. From him we learned that the schooner was called the *Dora M. French*, and that she hailed from Bangor, Me. The captain, the steward, and two sailors had gone down with the ship.

The *Portia* had also suffered considerable damage. Her foretopmast was dislodged and forty feet of rail lost. A hole was stove in the starboard bow just below the water-line, and the forward compartment filled with water. However, the damage was not serious enough to endanger her in any way. For an hour or so she lay to, and then slowly steamed onward on her way. Meantime her boats had been busy among the *débris* of the schooner, but not a vestige of the crew could be found.

At last, early on the following morning of September 11, we reached New York, and our remarkable trip was over. Within the short space of barely two months we certainly had experienced an extraordinary series of adventures. "Sweet is the pleasure after pain," and it is pleasant now to look back over the hardships and varied experiences that we encountered. Indeed, to have stood even at the outposts of the great and wonderful Arctic regions is ample compensation for the dangers and hardships that had been experienced. It is impossible to describe the beauties and revelations of these little-known regions—so different from the beaten paths of the ordinary traveller, or from any common experiences—that words are lacking in our vocabulary for any adequate description. Even the camera can do but scant justice; true, in a certain sense, but reducing vast expanses and towering icebergs and glaciers and snow-capped mountains to such microscopic proportions as to give but faint ideas of the real grandeur and impressiveness of Arctic scenery. Longfellow, in one of his finest ballads, tells how the noble Count Arnoldos, standing on the shore, beholds a stately galley steering toward the land, and hears the helmsman chant a song of the sea, wild and clear and wonderful :

> Till his soul was full of longing,
>   And he cried with impulse strong,—
> "Helmsman ! for the love of heaven,
>   Teach me, too, that wondrous song !"
>
> " Wouldst thou,"—so the helmsman answered,—
> "Learn the secret of the sea?
> Only those who brave its dangers
>   Comprehend its mystery!"

And only by braving the dangers of the Arctic regions can one comprehend their mysteries.

The season of 1894 was a particularly disastrous one for Arctic expeditions of any kind. Peary and Wellman and Jackson were all baffled by it; so little wonder if we did not attain, except partially, the objects of our much less ambitious enterprise. Since this disastrous season there has been a widespread cry of *Cui bono?* as regards Arctic expeditions in general. A senseless cry it is, coming from those who have given the subject no adequate consideration. There is scarcely a department of human knowledge that does not owe a deep debt to the baffled heroic men who have struggled to reach the Pole. They have given lessons to the world in patience, self-sacrifice, and heroic endurance. If as yet they have not attained their ultimate object, they have attained still larger results in extending the domains of science, of geographical knowledge, of civilization and commerce. If we justly honor our great historians, shall we not honor these men who have given us new chapters in a greater, larger history than that of man—the history of the world, the history of the universe? This material age should at least recognize the material benefits that have followed in the wake of Arctic explorations. The cod fisheries of Newfoundland, the whale fisheries of the Northern Hemisphere, the great fur industries, which have added millions upon millions of dollars every year to the wealth of the world—all these have been opened up by hardy Arctic explorers. But not yet has the world learned to appreciate the great work that has been done by the soldiers of science, or their bloodless victories, of vaster importance to the race than a Waterloo or a Sedan. The records of their victories are known only to the few, are unheeded by the many. The man of blood is still the world's hero. In England to-day the soldier who has won the greatest honors, and applause, and great wealth, has done little else than to slaughter some savage men and make them bow to a foreign yoke; but he has spilled human blood, and so his name has resounded from shore to shore. For, as in the old gladiatorial days, the thumbs of the cruel populace are still reversed, and the sacrifice of human blood is demanded as the price of its applause. Not yet have the great soldiers of science received their meed of appreciation; but when "the war-drum throbs no longer, and the battle-flags are furled," then will the world more fully understand the debt it owes to such men.

It is no vain ambition that leads the explorer into far northern latitudes, but a higher motive—a desire to comprehend the vast economy of this planet, to read its geological history, and to give the results of his labors to his fellow-men. Until the thirst for knowledge and the love of adventure is dead in the human heart, the Arctic regions will still attract explorers to its vast silences.

CAPTAIN DIXON'S LOG.

From August 16 to September 5, 1894.

NEPISAT, *August 16, 1894.*—About 4 P. M. came in to get a dory that we had landed here, intending to go to Cape Amelia. A native Eskimo came alongside, and by signs and broken English made us understand that we should go to Holsteinborg, that an American vessel had struck a rock and stove a hole in her bottom. After many questions he said it was an American man-o'-war. We took the kayak on board, and he showed us three letters. One was addressed to Captain Lawson, of schooner *Carrie W. Babson*, and the other two were addressed to captains of American fishing vessels. I opened one of these, and read the following letter from Dr. Frederick A. Cook :

"HOLSTEINBORG, GREENLAND, August 16, 1894.
"*To Captains of American Fishing Schooners.*
"GENTLEMEN :—The S.S. *Miranda*, carrying my expedition, with seventy persons on board, has struck a sunken rock coming out of Sukkertoppen ; she is now lying at that harbor disabled and in distress. Will you kindly come to our rescue? I am at Holsteinborg with five of the members of my party. Shall remain there until one week from date ; then return to Sukkertoppen. If this note reaches you in time to meet me at Holsteinborg kindly do so ; if not, come direct to Sukkertoppen, and send a note by kayak at once to Holsteinborg.
"FREDERICK A. COOK,
"Commanding."

I immediately made sail and started for Holsteinborg, but the wind fell off before we could reach the mouth of the fiord. Seeing that we could do nothing with the vessel, with a calm and fog setting in, I left the schooner in charge of my brother Will, to take her back to Nepisat, while I took a dory and four men to row to Holsteinborg, a distance of about eleven miles. We arrived there about ten o'clock at night. On entering the harbor we were greeted by the Eskimos, who informed us that Dr. Cook was at the governor's house, and we were escorted there by the entire settlement of Eskimos. I found Dr. Cook and his party, and he informed me that together with five Eskimos they had made the passage in an open boat from Sukkertoppen to Holsteinborg, a distance of ninety-five miles, or one hundred and forty miles, as they had to row it along the coast. They had arrived at Holsteinborg the day before, after a stormy passage of five days. Dr. Cook said that their steamship, the *Miranda*, of Liverpool, England, had struck a rock while going out of Sukkertoppen, and that there was a leak in her bottom that let the water into the tank for water-ballast; the tank had quickly filled with water, and the pumps could not reduce it. The ship would float as long as the tank could bear the strain of the pressure thus brought to bear upon it, but if the tank should burst the ship would sink immediately. Dr. Cook wanted a vessel to convey the passengers to some place of communication with their homes, and some one to accompany the ship to some place where she could be repaired. He had a letter from Captain W. J. Farrell, of the S.S. *Miranda*, which ran as follows:

"SUKKERTOPPEN, SOUTH GREENLAND, August 10, 1894.

"*To Whom it May Concern.*

DEAR SIR :—The steamer *Miranda*, of Liverpool, England, from New York, with Dr. Frederick A. Cook's Arctic expedition, struck a sunken rock seven miles southwest of this harbor. The ship is making water. Dr. Cook is going to you for immediate assistance, which please send, as we are in distress.

"Yours truly,
"CAPTAIN W. J. FARRELL,
"Master of S.S. *Miranda*."

As Dr. Cook had no authority to make a bargain that would recompense us for our loss sustained by leaving the fishing-grounds, or the risk that would be incurred by us in making a departure from our regular fishing voyage, I hardly knew what to do. Common humanity required that we should go to the relief of our fellows in distress, while on the other hand our voyage was likely to be a prosperous one if we stuck to our fishing. We had a crew of eighteen men, all on shares, and I felt as though they should have a voice in the matter before I would make any departure from our voyage. Sukkertoppen was ninety-five miles from Holsteinborg. The harbor was small, and the approach to it was encompassed by rocks. Our charts were little better than none. There were numerous icebergs all along the route, and a dense fog prevailed most of the time, with a very strong, irregular current setting along the coast, and in and out of the fiords. The land was strange to us (none of us having seen that part of the coast before), and if anything should happen to our vessel we should have to forfeit all right to our insurance on the vessel and the fish we had caught. I told Dr. Cook that I would go on board and consult with the crew, and if I decided to go to Sukkertoppen I would run up off Holsteinborg and set the flag for him to come off in his boat. We left Holsteinborg about 2 A. M., August 17, and arrived at Nepisat at 5 A. M. I called the crew into the cabin and explained the case to them, and asked them if we should go to Sukkertoppen. One of the crew asked me if I was willing to go, and I said I was. He said then, "I am willing to go, for you have more at stake than we have." That seemed to be the opinion of all the crew, and we got under way and started for Holsteinborg with a light air from the eastward. At 9 A. M. we reached the mouth of the fiord, and set our flag (being then about eight miles from Holsteinborg). Soon after leaving the fiord, and about two miles off of the land, we struck a sunken rock, and after bumping several times she came off, and we beat up off Holsteinborg. At 4 P. M. the boat came off, and we kept off with a good northeast breeze. At 8 P. M. the wind hauled to the westward with a strong breeze and a thick fog.

August 18.—Strong breeze, westerly. At 11 A. M. it cleared a little and we saw the coast. By 3 P. M. we had worked as far as Old Sukkertoppen. At 4 P. M. took in our mainsail and jib and set the storm trysail. At 8 P. M. took in trysail and put single reef in foresail. Had it rather rough for comfort during the night.

August 19.—At 8 A. M. the fog cleared a little and we saw land. Set the trysail and began to work down shore. In the afternoon it began to moderate, and we set the jib and single reef mainsail. At 5 P. M. set the staysail and flying jib. At 9 P. M. we were off Sukkertoppen, and we jogged off and on until daylight.

August 20.—As soon as it began to get light we tacked and made for the harbor. At 8 A. M. an Eskimo pilot came on board and informed me that I was inside of the sunken rocks and in a fair way for the harbor. Shortly after that we were met by a lot of native kayakers. There also came two boats belonging to the *Miranda*, in one of which was the master, Captain W. J. Farrell. I told Captain Farrell that I would for the sum of four thousand dollars take the passengers and carry them to Gloucester, or some place where they could get transportation home, providing they would furnish provisions. Captain Farrell and Dr. Cook informed me that they would furnish plenty of provisions, and that they considered the terms moderate and reasonable. So the bargain was accepted by Captain W. J. Farrell. Captain Farrell then asked me if I would accompany the ship to some port where she could be repaired. The object of this was to be ready to rescue the crew in case the ship should have to be abandoned. He thought that I could accompany the ship in the interest of the underwriters. I told him that I would do so, and we agreed to leave the amount of recompense to arbitration. Having arrived at the harbor, we dropped our anchor and hauled alongside of the *Miranda*, and began at once to make what hasty preparations we could to accommodate the passengers. During the afternoon I made out the two papers of agreements, and in the evening we took them to the governors' house, where we signed them, and they were signed, witnessed, and sealed by the Governor, and signed and witnessed by the Assistant Governor and the chief mate of steamer *Miranda*.

COPY OF ARTICLES OF AGREEMENT.—No. 1.

SUKKERTOPPEN, GREENLAND, August 20, 1894.

Whereas, The steamer *Miranda* being in a disabled condition, it is agreed between her master, Captain W. J. Farrell, and Captain Geo. W. Dixon, master of the Gloucester fishing schooner *Rigel*, that the passengers of the steamer *Miranda* be transferred on board the schooner *Rigel*, and carried to Gloucester, and that the crew and owners receive from the owners and agents of the steamer *Miranda* the sum of $4,000 as recompense for breaking up the fishing expedition of said schooner.

W. J. FARRELL, Master SS. *Miranda*.
GEO. W. DIXON, Master Schooner *Rigel*.
GEO. MANUEL, Chief Officer SS. *Miranda*.

Witness:
S. BISTRUP, Governor.
G. BAUMANN, Governor's Assistant.

COPY OF ARTICLES OF AGREEMENT.—No. 2.

SUKKERTOPPEN, GREENLAND, August 20, 1894.

Whereas, The steamer *Miranda* being in a disabled condition, it is agreed between her master, Captain W. J. Farrell, and Captain Geo. W. Dixon, master of the Gloucester fishing schooner *Rigel*, that the said schooner *Rigel* shall accompany the said steamer *Miranda* into some convenient port of repair. The crew of said schooner *Rigel* will hold themselves in readiness to rescue the crew and the officers of steamer *Miranda*, in case the steamer shall founder or have to be abandoned; and it is agreed that the recompense for such accompanying the steamer shall be settled by arbitration, or by mutual agreement between the agents of schooner *Rigel* and the underwriters of said steamer *Miranda* at the port of New York.

W. J. FARRELL, Master SS. *Miranda*.
GEO. W. DIXON, Master Schooner *Rigel*.
GEO. MANUEL, Chief Officer SS. *Miranda*.

Witness:
G. S. BISTRUP, Governor.
G. BAUMANN, Governor's Assistant.

At Sukkertoppen I found things substantially as the letter had stated. The steamer *Miranda* was an iron ship of between eleven and twelve hundred tons. She had struck a sunken rock off Sukkertoppen, and had evidently stove a large hole in her bottom, in a position where it let the water into the tank that was constructed to carry water-ballast, and the tank had almost immediately filled with water that forced through the hole. Thus the whole strain of the bearings of the ship upon the water was brought to bear upon the tank. A survey had been held and the vessel pronounced not safe to carry the crew or passengers. There were no means to repair the damage on the coast of Greenland, and the survey had shown that it was advisable that the passengers be transferred to some other vessel, and that some vessel should be secured to accompany the vessel to some port of repair, for if the tank should prove strong enough, the vessel would probably go safe.

In order to make room for the passengers, we took out about fifty hundredweight of salt, which we gave to the Eskimos, together with a lot of lumber and miscellaneous other things, to the value of about $85 altogether, and thus we obtained a space in the after-hold, on the salt, of about fifteen feet in length and twenty feet in width, and four feet in height. A door connected this with the cabin, and it was decided that the passengers occupy this space and the cabin, and that the crew should occupy the forecastle. We then spread sails on top of the salt, and mattresses on the sails, thus making snug but quite comfortable quarters, reaching forward to underneath the after-hatch. Forward of this was our fish, occupying a length of about twelve feet, leaving a space forward and under the main hatch of about twelve feet long, where we carried our water and provisions, and also our trawl and bony lines. This being completed, the passengers came on board on the morning of August 21.

In order to insure against a separation in case of a fog or in the darkness, we decided that the steamer should tow the schooner, so we used our one hundred and fifty fathoms of new cable as a tow-line, and arranged a few signals between myself and Captain Farrell, so we could have some little communication in case of need or accident. As we would require more room in case we had to take off the crew of the *Miranda*, we decided to put some of our trawl gear on board of the steamer before we left Sukkertoppen, so we put our sixty trawl anchors, valued at $43.20, and fifty-three trawl buoys, valued at $63, on board the steamer.

This finished our preparations, and we got under way in the morning of August 21, and with flags flying and the Eskimos cheering us and firing guns we proceeded out to sea with the passengers singing "My Country, 'tis of Thee."

August 21.—At 10.30 A. M. we took our departure from Sukkertoppen, and steered west by our compass. The wind was S. S. W., with a fresh breeze, and drizzly. We had our trysail and foresail set, and were making seven and one-half knots per hour. We passed numerous icebergs all day. The wind freshened until midnight. It blew a strong breeze then; fell off by 4 A. M. to a fresh breeze on the morning of August 22.

August 22.—Swell from south, with misty rain and indications of a storm at noon. The log showed 192 knots made since leaving Sukkertoppen, and I communicated this to Captain Farrell. By 7 P. M. the wind hauled to S.S.E., and increased to a moderate gale with a rising sea. At 10 P. M. a sea heaving in on our port side. Our vessel is crowded, we having on board sixty men, including our crew, and we have to keep off our hatch to get ventilation. The *Miranda* is carrying her lifeboats swung loose to the davitts, ready to drop them at an instant's notice. To-night the captain has a red light on deck. At 11 P. M. the wind seems to moderate a little. At midnight I hauled the log, and it showed 289 knots since leaving Sukkertoppen.

August 23. — At ten minutes past 12, midnight, the steamer *Miranda* sounded her whistle three blasts, that being the signal that she was in a sinking condition, and soon after they hung the red light over the stern as a signal for me to be ready. Captain Farrell slackened the speed of the *Miranda*, and as the two vessels came close together he hailed me to be ready, as he was in a sinking condition. I hailed him to cut our cable, and drop off in his boats, and we would pick them up. He said that he would try to hold by the steamer until daylight. There was a very heavy sea running from the southeast. Captain Farrell let the steamer come to head the sea, and when she was in the hollow of the sea we could see her masts at times. As soon as it was light he sent a boat with part of his men, and the boat then made three more trips, while we launched three dories that made from two to three trips each, thus taking off the crew and the officers and considerable provisions. Captain Farrell came off in the last boat, and before he left he cast off our tow-line, and the *Miranda* was soon out of sight in the dense fog. The ship was abandoned at 5.30 A. M. in latitude 61° 15′ N. and longitude 58° 40′ W. The barometer stood at 28.80 after the last boat came alongside of it. The crew and the officers of the *Miranda* numbered thirty-three men, making us ninety-three men all told, and in order to make room for them in the main hold I was compelled to take off the main hatch and throw overboard the remainder of our trawl gear, consisting of

32 sheets or bundles of trawl, valued at			$257.60
3,200 fathoms of bony line	"	"	32.00
1 oil barrel	"	"	1.50
With considerable rigging, etc.	"	"	15.00
			$306.10

Captain Farrell sent from the steamer two bundles containing silverware, and two chronometers, and two sextants, and some lanterns, and the crew saved their clothes. The silver, chronometers, and sextants, and the captain's clothing, were put in the cabin, but the lanterns were left on deck, because there was no room for them below. Captain Farrell and his crew were wet and draggled when they reached our vessel. I told the crew to spread their clothes in the main hold, so as to make a sort of field bed, and into this we packed all of the crew that we could put in, and then put on the hatch and barred it. After heaving in cable we made sail under our trysail and foresail and fore staysail and jib, and steered southwest, to try to gain Hamilton Inlet, on the coast of Labrador, that place being about 380 miles off. At 8 P. M. the wind died out, and we took in the foresail to keep it from slating to pieces.

August 24.—At 1 A. M. light air S.W., barometer 28.80, very heavy swell from S.E. Hoisted the sail, hauled the log, which showed 40 knots made since the steamer was abandoned. At 8 A. M. light air west, made sail and set mainsail and staysail, heading S.S.W. Barometer on 28.88. At 9.30 wind freshened to fresh breeze. At 12, log showed 76 knots. W.N.W. strong breeze. Got a peep at the sun this afternoon, which showed schooner to be in longitude 57° 55′ W.

August 25.—At 2.20 A. M. got latitude by North Star 58° 5′ N. Log on 95 knots. At 4 A. M. wind hauled southwesterly. Log on 5 knots, showing us to have made 205 knots since steamer was abandoned. At 8 A. M. wind S.W.; tacked ship in latitude 57° 40′, longitude 56° 45′. This is our first fine day, and the people are enjoying themselves sitting about on deck. There is a light air from the S.W., and but little progress has been made to-day. The barometer has been up to 29.50. At 6 P. M. the clouds show signs of rain, with frequent puffs of wind from the southward. At 8 P. M. it began to rain, and continued in floods all night.

August 26.—At 3.30 A. M. the wind ceased, and the wind hauled with a clearing sky in the westward. The barometer fell to 29.40. At 7.30 A. M. longitude by observation 56° 56′ W. The log on 30 knots; fine breeze northwest. At noon latitude by observation 56° 40′ N. Passed by numerous icebergs all day. In the afternoon the wind fell off and hauled to S.W., with light airs all night.

August 28.—At 8 A. M. sighted the coast of Labrador bearing W.N.W., and we took the liberty bell on deck and rang it; at noon got observation 53° 32′ N., and found the land to be Spotted Island. We had the wind S.S.W. and threatening weather, and decided to make a harbor for the night. We spoke a schooner and got a pilot from it for five dollars to guide us into the Punch Bowl Harbor, where we arrived at 5.30 P. M. and filled water before dark.

August 29.—At 8 A. M. light air from the westward, and we got under way and proceeded to sea, towing the vessel with dories until we were clear of the harbor at 11.30 A. M. Five of the *Miranda's* crew were left at Punch Bowl: the chief mate, Mr. Manuel; the pilot, Mr. Dumphy; the steward, Mr. Farrell, and two firemen. We had it moderate all day and night, with a dense fog. Saw the icebergs in the night. The day after we got outside of the harbor Messrs. Dove and Porter and Brown took a dory and, rowing among the fishing boats, procured a nice lot of fresh codfish, and we had a fine fish chowder.

August. 30—Calm in the forenoon, and light breeze in the afternoon. Thick fog all day. Passed numerous icebergs, some of them very close. To-day we discovered that the sailors of the *Miranda* had stolen our case of condensed milk, and I decided that, as a punishment, they should hereafter eat at the last table in the afternoon. We saw a great many icebergs, and at 5 P. M. we heard the breakers on shore, and we tacked and stood off.

August 31.—At 4 P. M. the fog scaled, and we saw Belle Isle bearing S.W. about ten miles. Saw a small schooner bound to Green Bay, N. F., and told it to report us. Strong breeze. We counted ten icebergs in sight at once. At noon we took a pilot and went into Henley's Harbor, paying four dollars to the pilot, which was raised by a tarpolan muster, and the passengers bought lots of fresh codfish, while I bought a barrel of herring. At 8 P. M. I went on shore, and had a fish dinner in company with Captain Farrell, Commodore Gardner, Dr. Vallé, Mr. Cleveland, Mr. Clover, Mr. Dewell, and Mr. Dibbs. Dr. Cook bought some provisions.

September 2.—The fog cleared off during the night, and as soon as it was daylight we got our pilot to take us out of the harbor. Got outside at 5.30 A. M. Wind west. Counted sixteen icebergs in sight at once just outside the harbor. At 9 A. M., calm. At noon the wind breezed out to westward, with rain. Passed a number of icebergs to-day. At 6 A. M., strong breeze E. by N. Took in mainsail and jib, and set trysail. Wind increasing. At 10 P. M. rope started off on the foresail, and we hauled it down and repaired it as well as possible, and put three reefs in it and set it, and then steered

W. by N. to smoother water, under the lee of the Labrador coast, as the wind was hauling to the northward. We had a very disagreeable night. Our stove would not draw, and we had to put the fire out, leaving it cold and damp and disagreeable. However, our passengers stood it like martyrs.

September 3.—At 4 P. M. we met a steamer going eastward; had a very sharp cross sea. Took in the trysail to let the stove draw, and built a fire in the cabin. At 6 A. M. shook the reef out of the foresail and put in a small reef. At 8 A. M. set the trysail and jib. At noon shook the reef out of the foresail. The wind being N.N.W., steered W.S.W. since 8 A. M. At 4 P. M. set mainsail and staysail, and set the course southwest, holding a good breeze all night. Last night Professor Brewer got a severe fall, caused by a lurch of the vessel that threw him on the cabin floor. Dr. Vallé and Dr. Cook attended him, and found some bruises, not necessarily serious.

September 4.—At 4 A. M. got latitude by North Star, 48° 13′ N. At daylight saw Cape Anquilla bearing S.S.E. At 9 A. M. saw Cape North, C. B., bearing S.W. Had a fine breeze until up with White Point. At 4 P. M. the wind fell off, nearly calm. At 8 A. M. we were off Ingamish Island, and the wind hauled to the S.W., with fog and rain that lasted all night.

September 5.—At 1 A. M. we saw Sydney light to windward, and after beating up, we entered Sydney harbor at 5 A. M., and got in and anchored about 7 A. M. Captain Farrell and Dr. Cook and myself went ashore, and I called at the residence of the Custom-house officer. He gave me permission to get any provisions that we might need, also permission for any of the passengers to go ashore to the hotels, which they were not long in doing, most of the passengers having declared their intention that they would go home by some other conveyance. At 2 P. M. the Custom-house officer came on board, and the passengers and crew of the *Miranda* were allowed to take their effects on shore. In the evening Captain Farrell and myself were invited to South Sydney, by the passengers, to a grand supper in the Sydney Hotel. I need not say that we accepted the invitation, and that it was a happy time that we could well appreciate after being huddled together as we had been for the last fifteen days.

ATMOSPHERIC DUST IN THE ARCTIC REGIONS.

BY PROFESSOR WILLIAM H. BREWER.

THE atmosphere always contains dust, and the phenomena relating to it have long been a subject of much interest to me. It is obvious that the air of the Arctic regions must be much less dust-laden than our own; therefore, during our trip to Greenland I made such observations on the related phenomena as were practicable without the use of special instruments.

The dust (including smoke) in the atmosphere is generally spoken of as an impurity or pollution. It renders the air less transparent, and is the source of various diseases and ailments of both mankind and animals. In this sense it is an impurity. It may also be so considered in the sense that it is not gas, but consists of solid particles suspended in a gaseous medium. In another sense it is not an impurity, but rather a permanent constituent of the atmosphere, always and everywhere present. It is also not an impurity in the sense that as a constituent of the air it plays an essential part in many meteorological phenomena. It varies enormously in its quantity, its fineness, its origin, its chemical composition, and in its effects, but is never entirely absent.

The relation of the suspended dust-particles to various atmospheric phenomena has been the subject of much recent study, and each year adds to its interest. It is scarcely more than twenty years since Tyndall showed its biological importance as being the active cause of ordinary fermentation and putrefaction, and also as causing the blue color of the sky. It is not yet fifteen years since Aitken showed the part it played in the formation of clouds, fog, and rain. Since then numerous observers have confirmed their conclusions and studied its relation to the colors of the sky, the nature of haze, and other atmospheric phenomena.

The systematic investigations have, however, been mostly restricted to work in laboratories or observations on the free air of a few regions in Europe and the United States, supplemented by casual observations on certain atmospheric phenomena observed elsewhere in the temperate and tropical zones. So far as I know, the recorded observations made in the polar regions are confined to the fact that dust has been found in the snow by several Arctic explorers. Captain Nares found it in the stratified snow over the "palæocrystic sea" in the far north, and others have noted it in the snows of Greenland and Lapland.

For a better understanding of the relations of atmospheric dust to certain phenomena in the Arctic regions it may be well to state a few elementary facts in physics and the conditions that exist in the other climates.

Watery vapor is a colorless gas and as invisible as the other gases are that constitute most of the atmosphere. It only becomes visible when condensed as cloud, fog, snow, or rain. Ordinary air will hold only a certain amount of this invisible vapor, the quantity depending on the temperature. When it contains all of the vapor it will hold at any temperature it is said to be saturated. If the temperature is raised, the amount of vapor required to saturate air increases, and on the other hand, if the air is cooled below the point of saturation a part of the vapor condenses as cloud, rain, or snow. The temperature at which it begins to condense is called the "dew-point," which is also the point of saturation. If it condenses on a large surface it is obviously liquid, but if condensation takes place throughout the mass of the air it forms a cloud, as always occurs when steam from a jet issues into the outer air. Until lately there has been much uncertainty as to the nature of this cloud. Some considered that the particles were hollow vesicles—minute bubbles, as it were—each containing a little air, and thus made buoyant. Others held that the particles were simply minute drops of water, so small that they were suspended in the gaseous medium, just as particles of dust are. In laboratory experiments on the matter the formation of cloud was found to be very capricious; sometimes it formed and sometimes not, and several curious hypotheses were suggested to account for the anomalies.

It was believed, however, that whenever saturated air was cooled below the dew-point condensation would and must occur, as it certainly did in free air. If it was on a cooled surface, then as dew; if throughout the whole mass of the air, then a cloud must be formed within the air itself; and if the supply of vapor was continued, or the temperature continued to fall, then the cloud-particles would increase in size and become drops of rain, or, if this occurs below 32° Fahr., then frost or snow. Such was the belief until a very few years ago.

It is now proved that steam or watery vapor does not readily condense unless it has a surface to condense upon. In the open air the suspended dust-particles furnish this surface. Air in closed vessels may artificially be freed from all dust-particles, and if a jet of steam be admitted into such an atmosphere no cloud is formed; the air becomes supersaturated—that is, contains much more vapor than it will hold in its natural state. It has thus been made to hold several times the normal amount required for saturation. If the smallest amount of common air (dust-laden as it always is) be admitted into such supersaturated air, cloud immediately forms. As Aitken expresses it, "dust is the germ of which clouds and fog are the developed phenomena."

Atmospheric dust is of very varied origin and fineness. A part of it is organic, coming from the vegetable and animal world, either as part of original growth or organic material partially decayed. Some of it consists of the solid particles in smoke ; a part consists of pulverized soil raised by the winds ; some doubtless comes from dust in space or the combustion of shooting-stars when they reach the atmosphere. These various ingredients are mingled in every conceivable proportion and are of every degree of fineness, from coarse drifting sands down to particles of molecular fineness. Illuminated by the sun or other light, the air becomes visible because of this dust. The rays are scattered, and diffused daylight and twilight are among the results. The particles may be so small as to break up the light-waves and by diffraction and polarization produce colors—reds, blues, greens, yellows, and their various combinations, according to the size and character of the particles.

Moisture begins to accumulate on these particles long before cloud begins to form, changing the color and visibility of the atmosphere, so the aspect of haze changes with the dryness of the air as well as with the size of the particles.

The sirocco of Egypt is a hot southerly wind from the desert, so laden with fine dust that it is an Arabian saying that it will penetrate the shell of an egg. Travellers describe the color of the sun seen through this air as red or dull purple. The harmattan is a scorching easterly wind blowing from the interior of the Sahara toward the Atlantic between Capes Lopez and Verde. It is so laden with fine dust that it is often described as a "dry fog," through which the sun appears of a dull red. It extends out over the Atlantic for nearly a thousand miles, and has been described by many travellers. It is much like the "dry storms" of San Diego County, California, which are hot, withering easterly winds coming over the intervening mountains from the interior deserts, intensely dry, and so laden with impalpable dust that the sun is seen through it dull and brown in color. The "dry fogs" of eastern California are of similar origin, and assume a variety of phases, according to the season.

The dry fogs, so called, which occur in many parts of the world, are composed of dust, not water. One extended over Europe for weeks in 1783, from the dust thrown out by the great volcanic eruption in Iceland that year. The great eruption of Krakatoa in July, 1883, belched forth dust for many days, and in such quantities that the coarser portions covered some of the neighboring islands several feet thick, smothering the unfortunate inhabitants. The finer particles were wafted around the world, producing effects that caused wonderment everywhere. In India the sun rose and set green for a week. In the Seychelles and in Brazil the sun was as pale as the moon. In Europe and the United States the most wondrous red sun-glows illumined the western sky a month or two later. We all remember them in the late November of that year. They extended to the Hawaiian Islands.

Civilization and agriculture add greatly to the amoun of atmospheric dust. The cultivated fields and the dry roads furnish much material, and the smoke produced in every house and manufactory adds to it. I explored the Rocky Mountains of Colorado before there were any railways or big cities there, and again a quarter of a century later, after it had become a great State, traversed by numerous railways, and when great cities had risen where I had only seen open plain or secluded valley. Farms covered the plain, and smoke rose from numerous smelting works and manufactories. During both visits I studied the atmospheric effect both from the valleys and from the mountain-tops to above fourteen thousand feet. The change in the atmospheric aspects produced by man was striking and obvious. The dust of civilization, the smoke from the numerous smelters, locomotives, and household fires, had so polluted the air that it was scarcely half so transparent as before, and had curiously changed the aspect of the landscapes when seen from the heights

No height yet reached by man is above this dust, but the higher we go the finer it is, producing corresponding effects. The intensely dark blue of the sky, the color often tinged with violet when seen from high peaks, is due to the fineness of the atmospheric dust at those altitudes. The coarser dust lies nearer the surface. Professor Langley has described it as seen from the summit of Mount Whitney, looking eastward over the deserts, and I have studied it from numerous peaks. The aspect varies with the season, with the weather at the time, and with the time of day. For illustration I may cite my experience on Lassen's Peak, in northern California. The first ascent was made when a cyclonic area was passing. An ocean of cloud was below us, driven by the furious wind and tossed into gigantic billows. We were entirely above this. Its surface was the purest white, illuminated by the sun from a cloudless sky, and eighty miles away the majestic curve of Mount Shasta rose a mile into the clear air above this cloud-ocean.

The next ascent was a few days later, after the storm had entirely passed, and illustrated the other features. This peak commands a wider view than I have seen elsewhere, extending in some directions to two hundred miles. We made the ascent in the night, and watched the marvellous colors of the dawn over the dusty deserts in the east. West and south of us was the great central valley of California, its objects clear in the early morning, but before midday it was filled with dust to the depth of a mile or more, shutting out all distant objects on the bottom. It was a hazy ocean with ill-defined surface and shores, shading into the mountains that rose above it on either side. The surface passed insensibly into that finer and clearer dust which extended into the upper regions of the atmosphere. At sunrise the shadow of the conical peak was visible, and the sun shining on the motes made the air visible on either side of the shadow, which was wonderfully distinct against the clear sky. It was of deep cobalt-blue, sharply contrasting with the light azure-blue of the sunlit air about it. By optical illusion this shadow seemed far higher than the peak itself. Owing to the curvature of the earth, it stood far above the mountain ranges on the distant horizon, a gigantic spectral peak projected against the western sky, sinking as the sun mounted higher, an object of indescribable grandeur.

Travellers have often described similar shadows of other peaks. Other optical phenomena occur, some due to the dust alone, others due to the partially condensed moisture on the dust. The Spectre of the Brocken, in Germany, and the glory about Adam's Peak, in Ceylon, are well-known examples.

The exquisite blue of the tropical skies, the dark blue-violet sky seen from very high peaks, the various phases of haze over landscapes, the charm of our Indian summer atmosphere, the green sun seen in India and in Ecuador after volcanic eruptions, the bloody sun of some climes and the copper sun of others, are among the optical phenomena due to atmospheric dust.

Our trip to Greenland was from the familiar atmospheric conditions of our own clime to those entirely new to me, and therefore had an especial interest. The ice and snow were not new except as to quantity and thickness. Much of the vegetation had a sort of familiar look; I had met so many of the same species on the alpine peaks of California, Colorado, and Switzerland. But the atmospheric aspects were new and strange, and at times fascinating. They showed themselves in the character of the rains and fogs, in the aspects of the sky and the landscapes, and in the mirages seen over the water.

The rains and fogs, and other atmospheric phenomena of that portion of the North which we visited, were just such as we might infer from the paucity of smoke and dust in the air there. Over the millions of square miles within the Arctic Circle practically no smoke is generated, and but little for many more millions lying in the high latitudes surrounding it. All the other sources of dust are scanty, and most of that which is wafted to the regions from more southern climes is washed out rapidly by the abundant rains and fogs. From the nature of the case, the difference between the air-temperature and the dew-point can never be so great as it is in our latitude.

It was evident from the character of both the fogs and rains that there was a paucity of dust-particles in the air for the water to condense upon. None of the fogs seen north of latitude 52° or 53° are so white and opaque as those which are common south of latitude 50°. There is much exaggeration in the popular description of fogs. We often hear them described as being so thick that nothing can be seen a hundred feet away. In fact, such fogs are rare, on sea or land. Comparatively few fogs are so opaque that large dark objects cannot be seen through them two hundred feet. I saw none in the Greenland seas through which we could not see several hundred feet, and usually very much farther. The fogs were all much more transparent than those we met with off the coast of New England and Nova Scotia on our voyage both out and back. They were, however, as a rule, very much wetter, and more misty. Often, when the fog was so transparent that we could see a half-mile, or even a mile, in every direction from the ship, the water would drip like rain from the rigging and every exposed surface, and our beards and clothes would be rapidly covered with fine drops.

Even those surface fogs which rested on the water under a clear sky, and which shut out the horizon, but with the sun shining through from above, were very wet. The ship's rigging, and even our beards, would drip, furnishing surface for condensation. On our return, and when in the dense, opaque fogs met with south of New England, I noticed the marked contrast in their wetness, so to speak. At times, when we could not see a ship's length, the air did not behave as if it was entirely saturated. The decks of the ship would dry after scrubbing, and other wet but exposed objects would dry even in the fog. The dust-particles in the air over these southern waters were ample to collect all the moisture, and more too; while in the Greenland fogs, condensation went on as if there was not dust enough in the air to supply the demand.

The fogs we met with in Vineyard Sound, before and after the collision with the schooner *Dora M. French*, were strikingly white and opaque, as contrasted with all those encountered in the Greenland seas, but were damp rather than wet.

All the rains observed north of latitude 53° differed from the summer rains at home in that they consisted only of small drops—mist rather than rain. For example, the heaviest rain we had at Sukkertoppen occurred on August 11. Numerous rills streamed from the rocky heights in small cascades, and streams poured from the scuppers of the ship, but the rain was a fine mist. It seemed strange that such misty rain, falling so noiselessly, could possibly wet so fast as this did. The same fact was noticed in numerous other rains, both in the harbor at Sukkertoppen and outside. In the heavy storm in Davis Straits, in which the *Miranda* was abandoned on August 23, and when the barometer fell one inch and a half, the rain, although very wetting, was a fine mist. This was in latitude 61° 15', and perhaps two hundred miles from land. Such was the character of all the rains we had while in the North, and on our return until just below latitude 52°, when during the night we had a shower of large drops. It was of short duration, but the patter of the big drops on the deck told us that we were back again to familiar atmospheric conditions.

The slight range of temperature was also probably a factor in the difference in size of the rain-drops as well as in the opacity of the fog. In warmer regions, we have not only a greater abundance of dust-particles upon which condensation may take place, but a greater range of temperature to promote rapid condensation. North of latitude 58° the surface waters were below 42° Fahr., and out over the open water the air was rarely above 46°. Often the difference between the air-temperature and that of the water was not over two or three degrees, and during the fogs in Baffin Bay the difference was usually less than six degrees, and local patches of fog would sometimes form with changes in the air-temperature of a single degree, or even less. In the fogs met with while in and near the ice off Cape Desolation there were sudden and temporary changes of one or two degrees of temperature in the air, during which there would be changes in the transparency of the misty fog.

The aspects of the sky and landscape were striking, and I think it probable that this produces—unconsciously, of course —one of the fascinations of Arctic scenery. The sky was a light blue, in the clearest day, and whitish in ordinary clear weather; yet the light was strong, and our professional photographer, Mr. Kersting, often remarked on its qualities for photography. Some of his views rivalled the best views taken in California, where the atmosphere is supposed to be especially favorable for outdoor photography. It is much more so than that of the Eastern States, yet, contrasting the atmosphere of the three, as to the physical characters, that of Greenland stands at the opposite extreme from that of California, and our photographs, as a whole, were strikingly good. There were nearly a score of cameras on board, and even the most inexperienced amateurs were brilliantly successful in getting good views.

During our detention at Sukkertoppen, awaiting the arrival of a rescue vessel, I made frequent trips to the surrounding heights, some of which commanded wide and exceedingly grand views. This is considered the boldest and most picturesque portion of Western Greenland. The headlands are lofty and precipitous, and the mainland and some of the larger islands are studded with pinnacled and inaccessible rocky peaks, furrowed by numerous narrow gorges containing more or less perpetual snow. The mainland is cut by three fiords, which run up the country for from forty to sixty-four miles. Beyond these are high and precipitous mountains, the higher ones being pinnacles of granite, with the great interior snow-cap surrounding them, and coming in grand glaciers down through the gaps between them to the fiords. The aspect of the region, as seen from the summits back of the colony, was impressively grand and striking.

There was absolutely no softening by blue haze, as we have over the landscapes of temperate climes. The sharp, rugged peaks rising from the desolate ice and snow of the interior, and the rounded, naked rocks nearer the sea, under the cold gray light had a scenic aspect very unlike any other landscapes I have ever seen. They had a sublimity of their own, which awed while it fascinated. They were indescribably impressive, but were not picturesque. The clouds which hung about the peaks much of the time were ragged, and had ill-defined edges. I saw none of the cumulus masses of cloud which constitute such a picturesque feature among the mountains of temperate and tropical countries. The clouds were usually stratus, and when not covering the whole sky had ill-defined edges, often fading off into watery mist.

When not wrapped in clouds or dim in the mist the rocky peaks were projected against a cold, gray sky. I have been told by travellers who have been frozen up over winter in the Arctic seas that as the sun leaves them in the autumn, and before it appears in the spring, there are very brilliant red sunset cloud-effects, but they were seen but sparingly during our visit. We had, however, the beautiful rosy "alpenglow" twice at sunset upon the great snow-fields and glaciers. It was, however, less pronounced than I have seen it on the snowy peaks of Oregon, California, Wyoming, and Switzerland. It is probable, however, that in the clearer and cooler weather of April and May the colors would be stronger.

Where there was any haze over the Greenland landscape it was a gray, watery haze, entirely unlike either the white haze sometimes seen over dry deserts or the blue haze seen over civilized lands and where there is smoke in the atmosphere. There was absolutely none of that blue haze which gives such a special charm to our own landscapes, where all the minor details are indistinct in the distance, and which produces such charming effects of color when the sun is low in the brilliant sky, glowing with yellow, orange, or red, as the case may be, the shadows of sunset fading from the glowing sky above into the indistinctness of the valleys, ending in a flaming red on the horizon above the spot where the sun has set.

We saw smoky haze in Labrador as we looked inland from the heights, but it was much fainter than in the regions farther north, and when we arrived at Sydney, on our return, the valley beyond the town was filled with it, the landscape fading into indistinctness in the blue distance; this effect seemed even more striking and beautiful than usual, from the contrast with what we had seen in the North.

The various forms of "ice-blink" and "ice-loom," so familiar to Arctic travellers, are also probably due to dust-particles or half-condensed vapor, scattering the light reflected to them from ice below the horizon. It is a peculiar color or appearance in the air which is above ice. The ordinary phases need no description here. We saw one little phase, however, which was so peculiar and striking that it may be noted. We had passed a very large berg, and were watching it carefully as it dropped astern to see how long it could be seen, but its actual disappearance could not be timed. A light spot hovered about it before it sank out of sight, and for some time after it sank below the horizon the place of its disappearance was marked by an illuminated spot in the air like a segment of a circle or an ellipse resting on the horizon, brightest near the water, and fading out from the centre.

Although not related to atmospheric dust, there is a phase of optical meteorology that needs, perhaps, a word. It is the mirage noticed by all Arctic travellers. We had our best example of that off Newfoundland and Labrador. In these regions the fogs occur when the winds are easterly, from the south round to the northeast; but the air clears when the wind is westerly or off shore. If it be mild and the air warm, then the mirage is likely to appear. July 16 was one of the most enjoyable days of the trip. We were steaming along the northeastern coast of Newfoundland, between latitude 49° and 51°. It was a clear day, with a very light wind off shore, and at times the air was so calm that the sea was almost glassy. The atmosphere was very transparent, and the sky overhead was brightly blue, becoming very pale toward the horizon. The sea-horizon itself was very dark, but not sharp; on the contrary, it was wavy and ill-defined, often ragged and changing in outline. We were in the great procession of icebergs coming down that coast with the cold current. These bergs were exceptionally abundant and large in 1894, and the effect of the distortions due to mirage of those on the horizon was fascinatingly beautiful. Distant bergs would be appearing and disappearing. Marvellous as their shapes are naturally, they were made much more so by this optical distortion, now magnified and lifted to many times their real height, then flattening out again, their wavy and flickering outline—bringing them into weird and strange shapes—continually changing in the brilliant sunshine. Sometimes they would fade out of sight, soon to be seen again peeping above the dark but capricious horizon, now divided into two with a belt of dark water between and then coming back to normal form or again disappearing entirely below the horizon, where a ripple on the sea showed that local belts of light wind broke up the unequally heated layers of air.

The mirages of these regions are nearly always the reverse of those seen on heated deserts, which I have often studied. Those are in the cooler air which rests on hotter soil. These are due to the warmer air resting on colder water, and the most common result is a "looming up," or bringing things above the horizon which would normally be below it.

This pure, dust-free air and cool temperature were peculiarly healthful. The hygienic effects were remarked by all our party, every one of whom returned in excellent health and strength, save one or two cases of minor accidental bruises.

I await with much interest fuller investigation on the atmospheric dust-phenomena of the Arctic regions. A quantitative investigation of the relative number of particles, and a comparison in this respect with the numbers found in other regions, are especially needed. Fuller and more systematic observation of the various related phenomena, made under other conditions and at other seasons, would be exceedingly interesting, and rich in scientific results.

GLACIAL OBSERVATIONS IN LABRADOR AND SOUTHERN GREENLAND.

BY PROFESSOR G. FREDERICK WRIGHT.

ON crossing Davis Straits from Labrador to Greenland one is deeply impressed with the contrast in the scenery of the two countries. The coast of Labrador presents everywhere a smooth and flowing outline against the sky. There are no sharp peaks, but everywhere the contour is subdued and graceful in outline. Upon the western coast of southern Greenland, on the contrary, the prevailing feature of the landscape, as seen from a distance of thirty or forty miles, is that of sharp, needle-like peaks, such as would do credit to the high Alps, or to the central portion of the Rocky Mountain range, though none of them rise more than 4,000 or 5,000 feet above the sea.

In seeking for the reason of this contrast one is at first puzzled by the fact that it is not due to any dissimilarity between the character of the rocks in the two regions, for they belong to the same age and are essentially alike in all respects, the prevailing rocks in both instances being gneiss, with occasional masses of granite and frequent intersecting veins of trap. We must look, therefore, for some other cause than the nature of the rocks for explanation of this diversity of appearance.

Due reflection upon the facts, and upon the forces in operation adapted to their production, will, however, furnish a satisfactory and adequate explanation. The flowing, graceful outline of the Labrador coast is the result of the horizontal erosion effected by such a rigid force as is furnished by an ice-sheet slowly moving over the surface and planing it down to a comparative level, while the coast of Greenland shows the signs of having been sculptured predominantly by the action of water and other sub-aerial agencies, rather than by an all-enveloping ice-sheet; for water erodes mainly in vertical sections, wearing deep, narrow channels at frequent intervals, leaving masses of land between the channels to be gradually worn by frost and wind and rain into the sharp, needle-like peaks characteristic of most high altitudes.

At first thought it seems improbable that the scenery on the coast of Labrador should betray the sculpturing power of a glacial ice-sheet more clearly than the coast of Greenland does, and the fact is of great significance; for there are no extensive glaciers in Labrador at present, while in southern Greenland great glaciers come down to the head of all the fiords, and some of them, as near Frederickshaab and Sukkertoppen, reach almost to the open sea; and everywhere the borders of a vast inland ice-sheet, thousands of feet in thickness, are met from fifteen to sixty miles back from the ocean. The question therefore arises with great force, Why is the scenery of the coast of Labrador more characteristically glacial than that of Greenland? The answer may best be given in a general statement arrived at by a number of separate inferences. Labrador was once more completely enveloped by ice than Greenland has ever been. The border of Greenland has probably never been completely covered by ice. However great the former extension of the glaciers, they were never confluent near the border of the sea, but flowed outwards in the separate channels now marked by the deep fiords, and were separated by numerous nunataks, or peaks, which perpetually lifted themselves above the ice, subject to the action of sub-aerial erosive agencies. If the margin of Greenland was ever, like that of Labrador, completely enveloped in ice, so as to be planed down to a nearly uniform level, it must have been at a period preceding by an enormous interval that of the glacial epoch whose evidences are now visible.

Yet upon penetrating the interior of Greenland to a distance of about twenty miles, where the margin free from ice is considerably wider than that, one sees before him the same characteristic flowing outline of scenery as that which has been described in Labrador. Instead of numerous sharp peaks, there is the subdued and gracefully rounded contour which would be produced by long-continued and general glaciation. Here, too, the other signs of a former occupancy by ice appear in increasing degree as one gets farther and farther into the interior. The summits of the higher plateaus above 2,000 feet bear the remnants of glaciers which were formerly much more extensive, and which even now send occasional projecting tongues of ice down to the lower levels, while frequent glaciated boulders dot the surface after the manner with which we are so familiar in the United States. But there is a remarkable absence of those extensive moraines and deposits of till or boulder clay which characterize the glaciated portions of the United States. This absence of extensive glacial deposits, characteristic alike of Labrador and of the interior portion of the outskirts of Greenland, points to a common cause.

Both Labrador and these portions of Greenland are so near the sources from which the supply of glacial *débris* has been derived, and they have been so long under the glacial harrow, that all the accessible loose material has been swept away to the margin, where the glacial deposits have been principally made. In both cases this margin of glacial deposition is covered by the sea, and hence is not visible. There can be little doubt that the submerged banks of Newfoundland are covered by deposits of glacial material derived from Labrador, just as northern Germany and northeastern Russia are covered with the waste from the Scandinavian mountains. If the continental plateau surrounding Newfoundland should ever be elevated so as to be again above the sea, it is quite probable that a vast population could spread out upon it and flourish upon the glacial grist of the Labrador mountains, as the southern part of Ontario and the northern part of the United States are now rejoicing in the fertility of the Canadian grist which has been so conveniently spread over them by the continental ice-sheet. There has been a remarkable movement in Germany recently in the direction of fertilizing the soils by grinding up certain rocks to powder and scattering it profusely over the surface. Eminent men have written to me concerning the feasibility of employing these kinds of fertilizers for our own soils. A convincing reply is readily made—namely, that nature has already done this for the northern part of the United States upon a scale which man cannot hope to equal. Every kind of rock from the north has been brought into requisition to furnish material for this glacial grist in the northern part of the United States, and the agriculturist has but to devise ways to extract its richness and his success is assured. But this process has left the far north barren of agricultural resources, even if the climate were favorable. Professor Helland estimates that as much as two hundred and fifty feet of material has been removed by glacial action from the Scandinavian peninsula and deposited over the surrounding belt of territory extending into northern Germany and northwestern Russia. There can be little question that corresponding deposits around both Labrador and Greenland are covered by the waters of the ocean.

At this point two inevitable questions may best be answered. First, were the glaciers of Greenland and those of Labrador ever confluent in Davis Straits, so that there was continuous ice between the two regions? This must be answered in the negative; for the evidence already given of the thinness of the ice over the outskirts of Greenland is inconsistent with any great extension of it from Greenland into Davis Straits, especially as the bottom, a short distance from the shore, descends rapidly to a depth of several thousand feet. This depth, together with the great width, which is here about six hundred miles, renders it extremely improbable that ice could ever have been supplied from the continent rapidly enough to have filled the whole intervening area

This leads to the second question, relating to the elevation of the land at the time of the glacial period. That the land on both sides of Davis Straits was much higher before and during the glacial period than it is now is shown by the great depth of the Greenland fiords and by the submerged channels through the Gulf of St. Lawrence. From the mouth of the Saguenay River to the margin of the Atlantic plateau two hundred or three hundred miles south of Newfoundland there is a well-marked deep channel through the Gulf of St. Lawrence several hundred feet, and toward the mouth from 1,200 to 1,500 feet, below the general level of the bottom of the Gulf and of the Banks. In other words, if that region should be elevated six hundred feet, the whole area covered by the Gulf of St. Lawrence and the Banks of Newfoundland would become dry land, intersected by a cañon from 1,200 to 1,500 feet deep, marking the ancient course of the St. Lawrence on its way to the sea. The inference is irresistible that in pre-glacial times that area was elevated to a height of from 1,500 to 2,000 feet; otherwise the erosion of such a channel is inconceivable.

The argument from the fiords in Greenland is of a similar nature. Their depth is such as to indicate a former elevation of the land to a height of several hundred feet at least. As they penetrate the interior to a distance, in some instances, of seventy-five miles, it would seem clear that the whole area must have been above the water-level at one time. In the case of the submerged channels through the Gulf of St. Lawrence the conditions are such as pretty much to preclude any other agency than running water as their producing cause. In Greenland, however, it is possible to introduce glaciers as the eroding agency in deepening the fiords when the level was very much the same as now, in which case we should not need to suppose any great former enlargement of the land area surrounding Greenland. In any case there is no evidence of the complete filling up of Davis Straits with land-ice; but, on the contrary, overwhelming evidence against it.

A more detailed description of my observations upon the Greenland coast during the summer of 1894 in the vicinity of Sukkertoppen will add considerably to the strength of these inferences. Sukkertoppen is in latitude 65° 25', and is the largest Eskimo settlement upon the coast, containing about four hundred natives, who find in its vicinity most favorable haunts for fish and birds, and for seal and reindeer. The general distance of the inland ice from the sea is here about sixty miles, which is the distance penetrated by Isortok fiord. But between Isortok fiord and Kangererdlugsuatsiak, which penetrates the outskirts to an equal distance, a projection of the inland ice extends to within about fifteen miles of the sea.

During our stay at Sukkertoppen in August I made two expeditions of much importance. First up Isortok fiord to about half its length, and again to the projection of the inland ice twenty-five miles north entering Ikamiut fiord. On both these expeditions there was abundant evidence that glaciers had formerly filled the fiord up certainly to a height of about 2,000 feet and extending out to the line of the ocean shore. In both Isortok and Ikamiut fiords the glacial scratches were very fresh and clear, distinct on all freshly exposed surfaces near the water-level, while upon the south side of Ikamiut fiord, facing the north, the glacial groovings parallel to the axis of the fiord were very distinct up to a height of 2,000 feet. Upon the side of the fiord facing the sun the alternations of heat and cold had caused the faces of the rock to crumble to such an extent that the markings were nearly all effaced; but upon the south side they were still very distinct, and could be traced up the fiord to the front of the retreating glacier.

Now that the main glacier has retreated for a distance of about eight miles up the whole length of the Ikamiut fiord, local glaciers are creeping down the flanks of the mountains at right angles to the former movement; and one glacier of considerable size is moving directly toward the front of the main glacier as it impinges upon the eastern side end of the mountain, thus showing how complicated are the movements accompanying both the advance and the retreat of the great ice-sheet, and accounting for the different directions in which glacial scratches often cross the same rock surface. It is evident that along this fiord from which the ice has retreated the local glaciers are furrowing and scratching the flanks of the mountain at right angles to those which were produced when the fiord was full of ice.

The glacier coming in to the head of Ikamiut fiord bore upon its back an enormous medial moraine, fed chiefly by branches from the north. This extended back as far as the eye could see, or until it was concealed by the freshly fallen snows. For the first five miles back from the front this moraine was fully half a mile wide, and contained many angular boulders from fifteen to twenty feet in diameter. Mingled with these, and with the sand, mud, and gravel accompanying them, were numerous perfectly rounded pebbles a few inches in diameter, showing the vigor of the superglacial streams which had doubtless borne them along from the distant interior. With so large a moraine upon the ice one would expect to find corresponding moraines in the area from which the ice had melted off; but their absence is readily accounted for by the great depth of the fiord, and from the fact that the moraine was very nearly in the middle of the glacier, which was here about five mile wide. The fiord is capacious enough to swallow all the material which the glacier has vomited into it.

Some years ago, when Nordenskiold visited the inland ice, a good deal was said about the dust which he found scattered over the surface, and which he surmised might be of meteoric origin. Dr. Holst, however, found similar material collected in considerable thickness over the margin of the ice all along southern Greenland, and ascertained, upon analysis, that it was simply dust blown from the mountains to the outskirts, thus furnishing a more prosaic explanation of the phenomenon. The fact that Nansen found nothing like kryokonite in the interior of Greenland confirms the conclusion of Holst, as did our own observations upon the Ikamiut glacier, which was covered with this dust, as we estimated, to a depth of a quarter of an inch, while in places it had been washed into hollows of the ice, filling them up to a depth of several inches.

Another evidence of the former extension of the glaciers to the margin of the ocean appeared in numerous light-colored granite boulders found at Sukkertoppen and other places, where the rocks were of an entirely different character.

One of the most puzzling things in southern Greenland is the existence of the reindeer; for it is difficult to see how the animal could reach those grazing-grounds under present conditions. It is not known that these animals make extensive journeys on the inland ice, or, indeed, that they venture upon it at all. Yet this projection of the inland ice that comes down to Isortok fiord would seem completely to isolate the grazing-grounds of the south from those of the north. The same difficulty arises in a still greater degree north of Umenak fiord, where for hundreds of miles there is now no margin of land uncovered with ice along the whole circuit of Melville Bay from Upernavik to Cape York; yet these animals are found in great numbers north of Cape York and all along the western coast south of Upernavik. They seem to flourish upon the abundant mosses and creeping herbage which grow in the protected nooks and crannies of all that inhospitable region, furnishing the most dainty food and the warmest of clothing to the hunters and their families.

The only way in which this distribution of the reindeer can be accounted for would seem to be by supposing that at a former time there was a broader and more continuous margin of land free from ice than there is now, and that subsequently this border was diminished to its present width and with its present interruptions, isolating different herds of the animal. There are two suppositions according to which this former enlargement and subsequent limitations of the border may have been produced. During a milder period the ice may have at one time retreated farther into the interior than now, allowing free passage along the whole border, and then at a subsequent time advanced again, as it evidently has done even much beyond its present limits.

The more likely explanation is that in the general elevation of the northern region which preceded the glacial epoch period a considerable border of the shallow ocean-bed was lifted above the surface of the water, affording extensive pasturage and free passageway all down the coasts of Greenland and of Labrador, thus facilitating the distribution of both animals and plants to the isolated localities in southern Greenland where they are found, and making it possible also for the various animals and plants to reach Newfoundland from the shores of the neighboring continent.

The mystery of Greenland and of the great ice age does not grow less as we extend our study of the facts, both past and present. When one treads the solitary wastes of the vast ice-fields of Greenland, they seem the very image of firmness and immobility; yet he has but to put his ear down to the surface to hear the busy hum of innumerable infinitesimal forces which are all conspiring to produce in their ultimate effects most startling results; and when once he returns to the head of the fiord, where the great glacier enters the sea, there is the most startling evidence of the irresistible power of these cumulative forces

THE GREENLANDERS.

BY FREDERICK A. COOK, M.D.

The aborigines of nearly all parts of the Arctic regions know no other name for themselves than "Inuit," the people. We call them Eskimos, or Huskies, but these names are as incorrect as the term Indians applied to our own wild predecessors. I shall here consider only a branch of the Eskimo stem, those who inhabit the Danish possessions of Greenland, a race of aborigines who have intermingled and intermarried freely with Scandinavians for nearly two centuries. This hopeless mixture has produced a hybrid population to which we can properly give the name of Greenlanders.

The Greenlanders are in every way inferior to the primitive stock, isolated hordes of which still remain beyond Melville Bay and on the east coast. In round numbers, the population is about 10,000, and for the past twenty-five years it has not materially increased or decreased.

Their present territory extends from Cape Farewell to the base of Melville Bay, on the west coast, and from Cape Farewell to Angmasalik on the east coast. The topography of Greenland is such that only the coastal fringe is habitable, and since the inhabitants obtain food and clothing principally from the denizens of the sea, their habitations are not far removed from the bleak and rocky shores of the relentless Arctic seas. There are several large indentations along the coast—arms of the sea, termed fiords—some a hundred or more miles in length, the shores of which usually have a fair share of population distributed over favored spots where game is abundant.

The climate of Greenland varies greatly with each locality. In the immediate vicinity of the open sea, the atmosphere is almost constantly charged with an abundance of cold moisture. Dense fogs are common throughout the year; but near the heads of the bays and fiords the opposite atmospheric condition prevails. There the winds are mainly from the ice-covered interior, and have been freed of moisture by cold; hence dry air, few fogs, and, in summer, a very agreeable temperature. The climate, on the whole, is by no means disagreeable to Caucasians. Indeed, some regions above Disco Island would form most excellent sites for sanitariums; for the effect upon nervous patients is marvellous. The natives, however, are badly fed, poorly clothed, and physically ruined by the misdirected charity of the Danish Government.

Contrary to the general belief, the people of Danish Greenland are less able to withstand the rigors of the Arctic atmosphere than are Scandinavians. Their wild elements of life have been largely supplanted by ill-adapted, semi-civilized habits which can only invite disease and destroy the people.

The soil, when it exists, is fairly fertile, and well moistened. In parts of the southern valleys a profusion of grass is found, and occasionally a small patch of stunted forest of birch and willows and other hardy trees, which grow to a height of from one to six feet. The agricultural possibilities are extremely limited, but there are many thousands of acres which would undoubtedly yield a fair harvest if properly cultivated. Next to nothing has been done by the Greenlander in this direction, and there does not seem to have been any effort to aid him. Indeed, the most fertile lands in southern Greenland are almost depopulated.

The animal life on land and water is rapidly vanishing. The wholesale slaughter of seals on the coast of Newfoundland and Labrador is partly responsible for the present scarcity of seals; but the disappearance of reindeer, foxes, and bears, and the diminishing bird life, are due to the introduction of firearms, and the indiscriminate destruction that always follows improved methods of killing game. With a fair amount of caution, there can be no doubt that even the present wild animal life of Greenland, and the adjoining waters, would supply a much greater population. If, however, the people were taught to domesticate reindeer, blue foxes, and bears, or import other fur-bearing animals, and carefully herd them, there would be no limit to the animal life that might thrive and multiply.

The Greenlanders encountered on the voyage of the *Miranda* were very fair specimens of the Danish Greenland population, their physical characteristics ranging from a typical Eskimo to a true Norseman. They varied in height from 4 feet 6 inches to 5 feet 7 inches, the average man being about 5 feet 5 inches high, and the woman 5 feet 2 inches. The pure-blooded Eskimo is about three inches shorter.

To the eye of the observer, the Eskimo is at once classed in a racial scale midway between the American Indian and the Asiatic Mongolian, and this is really his true position. Further acquaintance and more careful observation will lead an investigator into many puzzling moods, but he will always look at the Eskimos as a branch of the Mongolian stem. Their skeletons are the reverse of those of the negro. Their bones present ill-defined muscular ridges, short appendages, particularly small hands and feet. The skull is short and broad, the forehead very slightly retreating, the chin mildly protruding, and the molar bones are prominent. The nose is diminutive.

In studying a nude Greenlander, one is first impressed with the abbreviated appendages which the bony formation suggests, a great deficiency of muscular outline, and a very prominent abdomen. The men's skin is deficient in hair-follicles, and the women's is almost as barren as a bald head. The color of the skin varies from that of a fairly dark Caucasian to that of a Malay. The average Greenlander is perhaps darker than the true Eskimo. The skin has an amber or a light-brown tinge, with a deep-seated cardinal flush, easily sent to the surface of all parts of the body. Both sexes have very coarse and straight coal-black hair. To this rule there are very few exceptions, and they indeed are very odd—men with blond hair, blue eyes, and a dark skin, and to add to the unnatural aspect, they usually have light beards. They are unsightly and repulsive, but the few women of the same blond type are often remarkably beautiful. The prevailing face is broad, round, and beardless.

The chest of the child is fairly well developed, but that of the adult early loses its elasticity. The muscles of the trunk are very highly developed, particularly the erector muscles. Both men and women have great ridges of muscular tissue on each side of the spine. The body is enveloped in heavy integument, and considerable fatty tissue in prosperous seasons, but in this respect they have an inferior blanket of fat when compared with the most northern Eskimo.

Physiologically, the Greenlanders are the victims of circumstances: when food is abundant, nutrition is excellent and digestion is good; but when game is scarce, they seem to consume their own tissue, and become thin in proportion to the amount of fasting. They possess a remarkable ability to subdue hunger, and I have seen men and women subsist on next to nothing for a month and remain happy and contented. Their reproductive functions are good, but the infant mortality is great.

The prevailing maladies are principally the results of Danish sins, the frightful inroads of present diseases being quite recent; but their far-reaching effect bids fair to destroy the race. To the credit of the Danish officials it should be said, that they have tried nobly to prevent the introduction of foreign infection, but the result has been disastrous. The chief cause of death and the increasing fires of misery are the germs of tuberculosis. One physician told me that about two-thirds of the population were thus afflicted in one form or another, and according to my own observations, certainly the majority were consumptive. To show that the climate is not responsible for this, we have only to refer to the isolated Eskimo tribes, among whom the disease is unknown. Pleurisy, pneumonia, and catarrh are common, and all the zymotic diseases have prevailed. Skin diseases and disorders of digestion are very uncommon, while victims of gunshot wounds can be found in nearly every settlement. Broken and frozen limbs, death from land-slides, snow-slides, and drowning are frequent. Venereal diseases are almost unknown. The average longevity is very low, but Greenlanders who have reached eighty or ninety years are occasionally found.

The most interesting psychological characteristics are lack of common traits of character, a neutral religious aspect, though taught Christianity for more than a century and a half; great amity and compassion, a lack of courage, and an almost entire absence of hate and vengeance. Conscience, if it exists at all, is extremely elastic. The intellectual faculties are poorly developed, except such as enter directly into their peculiar life. Attention and observation are often found in abnormal proportions. The people are good imitators, and quick in making deductions and conclusions, but their imagination, contrary to what might be expected from a people living through long months of darkness, is very poor. The Greenlander's general disposition is congenial, friendly, honest, and affectionate, but his self-esteem is very low.

The language is a somewhat modified Eskimo tongue, and

is of the Anglutinated type. Its construction, though it seems at first sight simple, is extremely complicated. Many Danes who have married native women and have spent a lifetime in Greenland have only gained a working knowledge of the native speech. The difficulty in studying it is centred in the Eskimos' peculiar methods of constructing and compounding words which will convey an active meaning; hence, each word is a complete sentence, or a very large part of it, or perhaps a single word and a series of gestures convey a lengthy idea.

The question of language is a very long one, and from a scientific standpoint is very interesting; but it is difficult to analyze it without an overwhelming mass of technical details. The language is well adapted to the peculiar needs of the Eskimo people, but wanting in words to express advanced sentiments. It is rich and often extremely unique in expressions for seal-catching, dog-driving, blubber-eating, and animal sentiments, but quite deficient in definite expressions or accurate comparisons for things in general. Everything is either plenty or scarce, big or little, very great or insignificant. There seems to be no intermediate scale.

Morals are largely matters of convenience: one rarely encounters very wicked natives, and if judged from our standpoint, even more rarely very good natives. They are usually peaceful and mild-tempered, but jealousy or an infringement upon personal liberty arouses their worst passions. When a person behaves so badly that the community can no longer tolerate his presence he is forbidden to enter the huts, cannot share the food, or hold any intercourse with the others. Nevertheless, so long as he threatens no bodily harm, and displays no murderous intent, little attention is paid to him. He is ignored, and becomes a social outcast, which in this state of society is worse than death; it is the most effective punishment that an Eskimo can receive.

The virtues of the men are very much magnified at the expense of the women, and the wife regards her husband as her superior lord and master. Few men are jealous of their wives, but most wives are jealous of their husbands. The natural inbred admiration for men causes the women to treat all men affectionately. In this respect they resemble Oriental women, anticipating man's every desire, studying very carefully his needs and his follies. Chastity is quite unknown, and fidelity is uncommon; men treat the failings of the women with indifference—wives are exchanged and new attachments are made as a most natural and necessary function. Both men and women are prized not for beauty, physical force, or wealth, but for their ingenuity in the arts of life. There is among them a large idle and non-productive class, but this is not criminal or dangerous, as is the rule among us.

The product of the hunt furnishes the natives with food, fuel, and clothing. The Danes supply them with some unnecessaries, such as tobacco, coffee, sugar, salt, superannuated biscuits, cloth, etc.; but the people would be much happier and healthier without these things. This is particularly true of tobacco and coffee, for there seems to be something in the atmosphere which forbids the use of these stimulants and makes them quite as destructive to ambition, respectability, and health as alcohol does among our working classes.

At their feasts there is much eating and merrymaking, but the time devoted to them is brief, and the fun never ends in fighting; but there is sometimes an exchange of wives, and more or less free love. Their life is essentially one of periodical wealth and poverty, of boundless engorgement with alternate starvation, but they move about from day to day, and from month to month, with no care for the future—happy alike in famine and in luxury.

My companions, Messrs. Walsh, Dewell, and others, have

mentioned other interesting traits of these people, which they have observed in their own way. The natives, like the landscape, appeal differently to every imagination. The unique and quaint little characters, and the bewildering, strong, relentless scenes, incite the mind, but throw it back upon itself. They inspire the imagination, without satisfying its curiosity. Every intruder into Greenland solitudes, and every student of the people and the animals, has found the life and the air charged with interest, and every inquiring mind has been filled with an endless mirage of fascinating perspectives. There is here a clear view of primeval nature, seen through the crystal lens of rarefied air. We have a clear understanding of prehistoric life, born of an easier study of simple nature, in its wildest elements. The method and the time may be forgotten, but the inspiration and the place will ever remain in our memory.

It is to be hoped that the future will bring new arts, an extermination of diseases, and a better adaptability to the stormy conditions, to these unfortunate people. They cannot long remain isolated from civilization, because they are perched on the shores of the world's most interesting landscape, which will always be an increasing point of interest. The coastal fringe of Greenland, with its people and its life, is the most sublime and magnificent cyclorama of nature; its superb mountains, towering terraced cliffs, chaotic abysses, great sheets of spotless snow, endless stretches of glacial ice, and numberless silvery threads of winding waters have no equal. It is a region of incandescence in summer and glowing blackness in winter. It fills the soul of man with awful despair and violent delights, extremes which, like the coastal mountains, are separated by great gaps.

A GREENLAND CEMETERY.

BY JAMES D. DEWELL.

WITH Melville Bay as the objective point, I boarded the steamship *Miranda* July 7, 1894. After many delays caused by fog, collision with an iceberg, and striking a hidden reef, we anchored in the little harbor of Sukkertoppen (Sugar-loaf), Greenland, in early August. Sukkertoppen is a settlement of four hundred Eskimos, under the Danish flag, a race without a history or a nationality, a people of Asiatic caste, whose progenitors were probably from a warmer clime. How came this peculiar people to inhabit a frozen region can only be surmised. The belief is that in ages past their ancestors were forced north by tribal wars, probably before the date of the English Channel, and thence through some emergency reached the north coast of Greenland, when that portion of the earth's surface was more temperate than now. As the cycles of time rolled along, and the ice-fiend claimed pos-

No. 1.—CEMETERY LOOKING NORTH.

session of all that is now known as the great ice-cap, this remnant of a once important tribe worked their way down the coast to Davis Straits, where they now struggle in poverty for existence.

While waiting for relief, a matter of two weeks, we examined the settlement and its surroundings. My first thought

NO. 2.—CEMETERY LOOKING SOUTH.

was, in case of death where might we be buried? but in any event I desired to see the place where the Sukkertoppeners buried their dead. Their method of burial is not as they would have it if living in a more favored clime, but is caused by the conditions of climate and surroundings. Disposition of the dead has been from remote times mostly a grave subject. The ancients had a way of embalming and depositing their dead in tombs; hence the mummies. The origin of mummification in Egypt has been much discussed, but it has been proved that the preservation of the human body was deemed essential to the corporeal resurrection of the dead.

Cremation in a rude form among certain other ancient peoples was also practised. To-day in India some deposit their dead in the water, and the Parsees leave their dead on the roof of a mausoleum or chapel, where the cormorants or birds of prey eat the flesh from the corpse. In other portions of the globe the dead are placed in trees or on poles. It remains for the poor Eskimos of Greenland to show to the civilized world that the dead may be buried without even digging a hole in the ground.

No. 3.—OPENING A GRAVE.

In Greenland, cremation, or earth-covering, or embalming, is utterly impossible, and, owing to the climate, quite unnecessary. The views of the cemetery at Sukkertoppen which accompany this article were photographed by the writer in August, 1894. No. 1 represents the cemetery looking north up the fiord, with the great ice-cap and snow-mountains in the distance, forty miles away or more. No. 2 shows the cemetary looking south toward Davis Straits. It is a large plot in a cañon, the rock projections exhibiting deep glacial marks. No. 3 shows a party opening graves to collect specimens for scientific purposes. No. 4 shows wooden enclosures, and No. 5 the Lutheran church. All of the Eskimos south

A GREENLAND CEMETERY.

of Melville Bay are Lutherans, having been Christianized many decades ago by Danish missionaries. I found that they were poor in all things except good nature, and were especially poor as to a suitable ground whereupon to deposit their dead, there being no soil or vegetation in all that section. Our two weeks' stay gave us ample opportunity to visit the natives in their homes, which are simply squalid huts, but no chance to see a funeral. However, I visited the cemetery, and found that as there are no trees there can be no wood, and consequently, no coffins. The only wood is either brought from Copenhagen or caught from the drift. The

No. 4.—WOODEN ENCLOSURES.

dead, wrapped in sealskin, are simply laid on the surface of the rocks. (Hair seal is the mainstay of the natives: skin for clothes, flesh for food, fat for light and heat.) The body is then covered to the depth of perhaps ten inches with moss scraped from the sides of a friendly rock, over which are mounded stones of various sizes to keep the body from wild beasts, and serve as a monument. In examining illustration No. 3 the reader will observe that the graves are simply stone mounds. We found in all of the old graves only skulls, securing five in good condition in one mound, and no other bones. A fine collection was gathered, but it went down with the *Miranda*.

There are exceptions to the average mound, as may be noted by illustration 4. The Danes, who are in control of all the Greenland coast below Melville Bay, have a wooden enclosure surrounding their graves, the wood being brought from Denmark; and wooden crosses mark the graves of the more favored or better portion of the

No. 5.—LUTHERAN CHURCH.

Eskimos. All the other graves, filled with the poor, simple children of the frozen north, have no other monument than a heap of stones, which in a later day is overturned by some explorer in search of human frames in the interest of science. This brief article cannot give the reader my thoughts fully as I contemplated this God's acre. Here are the bones of human beings, some of them, perhaps, descendants of kings from southern climes in centuries past, and beyond the memory or history of the living. It was noticeable that the mounds exhumed brought to light mostly skulls, furnishing evidence of antiquity, as being probably of those who died before the Lutheran missionaries landed here. Yet the method of burial remains as before, even though the present generation is blessed with religious rites. The people on the western coast below Melville Bay are all nominally Christians, and dispose of their dead in the same manner as at Sukkertoppen.

It has been frequently asked, "Why do the Eskimos remain in the frozen region?" The answer is plain and simple. They know not of the outside world, and withal have neither the desire nor facilities to leave their bleak and desolate habitation. To bring such a race to a warmer climate and to civilization would insure its entire extinction. The future of this side-tracked race can only be imagined. My opinion is that ere many decades it will become extinct.

THE ESKIMOS' TEETH, AND OTHER NOTES.

BY R. O. STEBBINS, D.D.S.

To VISIT the far north, for the purpose of studying the character of the Eskimos, I joined Dr. Cook's Arctic expedition of 1894.

Although our vessel was abandoned at sea, and all our baggage and curios, such as skin and bone trinkets, clothing, made by the natives of furs and raw hide; cider-down from the duck, and other bird skins, together with implements of the chase, the kayak, oomiak, and sledge-snowshoes, etc., were all lost, the memory of those curious little people is fresh in our minds, and not likely to be obliterated by time. Nor can we forget the grand mountains of rock, void of earth and shrub, the beautiful fiords, dotted here and there with many islands, mere rocky peaks, penetrating from the fearful depths below; the eternal ice-cap of that glacial continent, with its mighty rivers of ice, forcing their way down through the rocky cañons, depositing great masses of ice in the fiords, with a crash and splash that can be heard for miles.

The waters of the fiords seem to afford a great quantity of nutritious seaweed and small fish, upon which feed the millions of birds—gulls, ducks, and geese. The birds nest so close together along the crags of the rocks that they look like patches of snow.

The Eskimos are very fond of eggs, and will sometimes lay in a supply for the long Arctic night. This is done by stripping the secretions out of the gut of a seal and refilling with the eggs, which they break and pour in, tying up the end of the gut. It resembles a gigantic frankfurter, and freezes solid when the cold weather sets in. The natives break off bits with their teeth, swallowing them uncooked with a relish. While camping out on the moss-covered rocky banks of a river which runs into one of the fiords, I caught with one little artificial fly two hundred and twenty salmon-trout, varying in length from six to eighteen inches, landing one hundred and sixty-two in one day from a pool formed in the bend of the river, beyond which the water ran very swiftly. Allowing the fly to disappear in several feet of water, I found the fish to be quite game, as often a small one would make you think a ten-pounder had taken hold. All hands ate the fish, which were fried in a skillet over an oil-stove, with great relish, except Dr. Cramer, who did not care for fish, and as we were short of bread and limited to one piece, I gladly forfeited my portion in favor of the Doctor, and filled in on fish.

While returning to Sukkertoppen in an old, leaky boat, loaded with the tents, cooking utensils, and camp traps, together with three Eskimos to row while I handled the tiller, I discovered that a few crackers, my supply of provender, had become soaked in dirty bilge-water. After sitting in a cramped position for sixteen hours, cold, stiff, and damp, from the spray of the waves, which were tossing our boat around in a lively manner, I was getting pretty hungry, but could not make up my mind to tackle the dirty crackers. Presently I noticed one of the Eskimos eating raw salmon that had been cleaned and partially dried on the rocks before leaving camp. It was of a rich color, and looked very tempting. I asked for a piece. He pulled out a salmon, or rather half of one, from an old filthy sealskin, which is a garment worn by the Eskimos in stormy weather and used as a travelling-bag when off duty. I trailed the fish overboard (which caused my companion to smile), and then let it dry, and began to pick at it. It was not bad; in fact, I thought it very good before I had eaten the entire piece (about three pounds), and realized how easy it would be to fall into the habit of eating the uncooked food as the Eskimos do.

Before leaving New York I purchased ninety dozen Seed's dry plates for my camera from E. W. Newcomb & Co., and twenty boxes of their developing powders. On our trip north, in Labrador and Greenland, I had exposed three hundred and ninety-two plates and developed them on shipboard, making a dark room of our stateroom.

The loss of these plates, of course, I regret very much; but the greatest loss to me was the casts I had taken, twenty-eight in number, of the Eskimo teeth, from childhood to old age. Duplicates of these casts I expected to place with others I have in the National Medical Museum, at Washington, D. C., as there they could always have been referred to in the scientific study of the teeth.

Years ago it was reported by sailors that the Eskimos had double teeth all round—that is, the front teeth looked the same as the back ones. It did not take me long to discover the reason of this report. Upon observation, as a dentist, I ascertained that the incisor teeth, also the cuspids and bicuspids, were worn off blunt. As these teeth were large and prominent, they did not look unlike molar teeth.

The older natives live entirely on fish and flesh uncooked, and they do not chew their food, but swallow it like a dog. This accounts for the way their teeth, as a rule, articulate, square on the end of the incisor teeth, the molar teeth not being used at all as masticators. In preparing bird and other skins, the natives chew or work the skins between their front teeth, sucking out the oil, tearing off bits of flesh and fat, and making the skin very soft and pliable. As their teeth are rather soft, more like ivory in color and texture, the manipulating of the skins wears them off a great deal. Very little decay was observed in the mouths of the original natives. The present generation of Greenlanders, or Danish Eskimos, since the introduction of the cook-stove and breadstuffs by the Danish Government, cook most of their food. Their teeth are more brittle, and the incisor teeth are not worn off so much, for their molar teeth are used to masticate the cooked food, while the aborigines subsisted entirely on raw food. Their upper incisor teeth project over the lower ones. Decay was observed in the six-year or first molar teeth, while not a sign of decay was discovered in any other teeth of the same mouth.

Some of the present generation are also fond of raw food as well as cooked. While fishing up the fiord, a little fellow asked if he could eat one of the fish I had caught. I gave him one just taken off my hook : he held it by the head, bit off a piece and swallowed it, then another, until the fish stopped wriggling and he had eaten or swallowed the whole.

The eyes of the women resembled those of the Chinese. They do their hair up very tightly on the top of their head, and always wear it in the same way, from childhood. This draws the skin very tight over the temples, and as they squint at the glare of the sun during the long Arctic day, their eyes grow on a slant. The men have small, sharp round eyes, and their hair hangs long and loose about the head and face.

THE FLORA OF SOUTH GREENLAND.

BY SAMUEL P. ORTH.

ON the bare rocks and bleak hills of the far north everything that has life is of peculiar interest. The beauties of the Arctic flora can nowhere be surpassed in daintiness and exquisite tintings. There is no useless flaunting of colors or gaudiness, but a pure, transparent tint which brush cannot reproduce.

There are several circumstances which combine to make the floral life of Greenland very interesting and simple. The short summer makes it necessary for all the species to bloom at one time, there being practically no succession of flowers. The soil is shallow, thus affording little opportunity for sprouting. The pure atmosphere, free from dust, contributing so much to Arctic landscape and sunset, tells also on the pure colors of the flowers. The long day and very short night of the summer make a double share of the sun's actinic rays possible to the plants. This accounts for the rapid growth of vegetation. All these circumstances create the beautiful delicate forms which so surprised us all on our mountain climbings.

Everywhere along the coast lichens and mosses share their tints with the landscape. The peculiar dull-red glow of the islands and rocks is caused by a moss-like fungus covering the ocks everywhere. Farther in the interior, lichens thrive in myriad species. Never before had I seen such a profusion of fungi as on those cold Greenland rocks. In the pools of the valleys mosses thrive most luxuriantly. Especially beautiful is the sphagnum, with its lighter tints, growing with dark-red varieties in the crystal pools of mountain streams.

But the phanerogams are the most interesting to the ordinary visitor. Nowhere can the persistence of life be more closely studied than in these bleak regions. Wherever there is an inch of soil, in every crack or crevice, thrives a plant. From the deep valley to the snow-line, nature has prepared a succession of surprises for the flower-lover. In the lowlands, pink saxifrages and yellow buttercups thrive with our own dwarf cornel (*Cornus canadensis*) and the pretty gold-foil (*Coptis trifolia*). The grass plots are dotted with the golden Arctic dandelion (*Taraxacum arcticum*). Fringing the hillsides, grow the forests of willows and birches (*Betula nara*). The willow is the largest Arctic shrub. Several varieties abound, all common, all trailing around the ground or over rocks. The largest one I measured was three-quarters of an inch in diameter and seven feet high, including four feet of roots. With the willows and dandelions grows the common polygonum, perhaps the most abundant of Arctic plants, and the banks of the streams are lined with chickweed (*Cerastium*) which, in all of its several varieties, has exceptionally large flowers.

Farther up the mountain-side, in the lighter soil, beautiful red primroses and delicate bluebells greet one, while in sandy spots the gorgeous red stonecrop (*Sedum rhodiola*) presents a startling contrast to the usual blues and whites. This stonecrop is the most extravagantly colored flower of the North. It is often seen clinging to the perpendicular rocks, hundreds of feet above the water-line, as you row along the fiords.

The blueberry was perhaps the most welcome plant found. I saw here, bud, blossom, green and ripe fruit, all on one bush. It is scraggy and low, but the ripe berries tasted so civilized! In all books of Arctic travel one reads so much of the Arctic poppy, with its flaunting yellow petals. Naturally I searched for the plant, which is so abundant farther north, but I found only one plant, with a bare seed capsule, the petals having fallen off.

Rarely one finds a low juniper with green berries, the climate being adverse to the ripening of the fruit. Grasses are confined to a few species. A small, pretty festuca is the most common, making a pretty lawn on every level plot, and often appearing in feathery tufts in the crevices of the rocks. A large, barley-like grass, growing along the sandy beaches, is the largest grass found. It grows about two feet high.

Of special interest is the angelica, thriving luxuriantly in the ravines and lowlands, in sheltered places. It is the only vegetable known to the Eskimo's palate, and is gathered in large quantities, but never preserved for winter use. It grows about eighteen inches high, and has the peculiar flavor which characterizes so many umbelliferæ and makes them a favorite dish with us.

There are but few varieties of ferns, all growing in sheltered places, behind rocks. The commonest is a pteris, and occasionally one sees an ophiaglassum and aspidium.

It was intensely interesting to note the gradual change of flowers as we stopped at various places along the coast. Our own flora was little modified at Cape Breton—only the flowers were about three weeks later than in southern New York. Newfoundland added several new species, including the pretty forget-me-not, while Labrador's flora was entirely new, and quite introductory to the Greenland flora.

Of the Labrador plants, none of us will forget the "curlew-berry" which grew everywhere so abundantly (found in

Greenland also), and the "bake-apples" which so refreshed us on our homeward journey when we stopped at Punch Bowl.

As the collections were all lost, it is impossible to give an accurate list of the plants collected in Greenland, though I had prepared a list of those found in Labrador. A safe estimate made from my notes is the following: Phanerogams, eighty, including five graminæ and ten cyperaceæ. Of the pteridophytes, I found one equisetum and three filices—making a total of ninty-eight plants, excluding the mosses, fungi, and lichens, of which there are many dozens of species. The most complete works on the flora of South Greenland are the Danish Government reports, which are often quite full and interesting.

NOTE ON THE INSECTS OF SUKKERTOPPEN.

BY L. J. W. JOYNER.

OWING to the loss (together with note-books) of my collection of insects, of which a very fair number had been captured, no attempt at any list, much less a classification, can be made. The field appeared to offer good opportunity to the entomologist during the prevalence of the brief heat of summer. Though coleopterous insects were expected in some abundance, a most careful search revealed only a few specimens. On the other hand, many species of the order *Diptera* simply swarmed, and more than one species of the genus *Culex*; but a single species of mosquito, considering the swarms in which they occurred, would have been quite sufficient to arouse the keenest interest of an average or casual observer. Acting on the principle of "Live and let live," I always make a point of never disturbing a mosquito at his meal ; but in Greenland I was absolutely brutal and unreasonable. Most of us can testify to the fact that, in spite of the cooler climate, and the consequent harder conditions of their life up there, these mosquitoes were by no means slothful. Some of the flies, too (particularly when one was busy fishing), left one's face smeared with so many vertical lines of clotted blood that it had to be scraped before recognition could take place. I made several fine collections of this species, but do not regret their loss. Among the *Lepidoptera* were observed about a dozen species of *Heterocera* (many of them day-flying), and of the *Rhopalocera* (butterflies) two species appeared to be tolerably common—one a colias and the other of the genus *Argynnis*. The order *Hymenoptera* was represented by a good number of bees, humble-bees, and ants, and many species of ground spiders were phenomenally plentiful. *Pulex gigäs*, they say, occurs in Greenland, and nowhere else, but I kept away from the Huskies.

THE FINDING OF THE RIGEL.

BY RUSSELL W. PORTER.

AT THE time the boat journey up the coast in search of assistance was decided upon matters relating to the party's welfare were in a very bad way. As far as we could make out, from what we already knew and from what we learned from the governor at Sukkertoppen, our chances for returning to Europe or the United States that summer were very slight. No more Copenhagen trading vessels would put in at Sukkertoppen, and Captain Farrell, of the *Miranda*, said she was not safe to return in unaccompanied by another vessel. So our only chance was to intercept and bring to our relief one or more of the American fishing schooners which were usually to be found about this time somewhere off Holsteinborg, near the Circle. Holsteinborg was one hundred and forty miles up the coast, and with a fair wind could be reached in a few days.

So the open-boat journey was decided on. Dr. Cook unfolded his plans to us in his cabin. In the party were Ladd, Thompson, Rogers, Dunning, and myself. He frankly told us what we might expect—hard work at the oars, bad weather, camping on the rocks, etc., but we determined to go, some of us being glad to get the chance.

The governor was kind enough to give us the use of his twenty-one-foot whale-boat and a large tent. To these were added provisions and bags and a crew of six Eskimos, one of whom was a full-fledged "kayaker." We started at five o'clock on the evening of August 10, leaving the crippled ship amid the cheers and good wishes of our comrades. We were soon in our oilskins, and on rounding the point at the mouth of the harbor we turned north. The two spritsails were set, and we were fairly off on our hazardous journey.

We were cramped for room; provisions, sleeping bags, tents, and eleven men brought the gunwale uncomfortably near the water's edge, especially when we got the full force of the wind while crossing the mouths of the fiords, and the tops of the waves came into the boat. The scene opening up to us was grand and awe-inspiring, similar to what was seen by the rest of the party in their trips about Sukkertoppen. Realizing, as we did, the seriousness of our mission, it made a deep impression on us. As night, or rather twilight, dropped down about us, and the mountains far up the fiords were reflecting the last red rays of the almost midnight sun, the bold rocks and headlands we were passing stood out in all their savage beauty. The sharp guttural "uk," "puk," "tuk," terminations to the Eskimos' warnings, as they saw the squalls coming, were weird and unnatural.

This ever-varying scene of rugged mountains and islands, of the inland snow and the majestic fiords, was present during the entire trip. We saw it in all the lights and moods that nature alone could give, from the clear, sharp days when the fog-bank rolled out to sea and the clouds lifted from the mountains, showing us the shimmering ice-cap far inland on the horizon, to the days of wind and rain, when, storm-bound on some unknown island, we watched the black cliffs frowning down at us through the mist and rain.

Our run the first day was forty miles in eight hours, arriving at half-past one at Kangarmuit (Old Sukkertoppen), where we were greeted with a most unearthly chorus of howls floating out on the morning air. That night we slept in the attic of the church, and glad we were to do so, for it saved us pitching the tent. The next day, being rainy and "plenty [too much] wind" outside, we spent with Chief Trader Rosin, drinking coffee with him and trading with the natives.

We started on Sunday morning, with the entire populace at the shore to see us off. A stiff, fair wind favored us, and by eleven o'clock that night we had another forty miles to our credit. About noon of that day we passed "Upper Strun" fiord, the largest in western Greenland. It runs inland over a hundred miles.

Camp Raven, named from the fact that two ravens croaked over our tent all night, was broken early Monday morning; but such a wind was blowing that before we had made a mile northing Dr. Cook gave directions to put back to shelter. And high time it was, for as we were pitching the tent the storm broke, and for two days and nights it continued with such fury that it was seldom we ventured out. I never knew what a "blow" was till the wind came down off those mountains and tried to carry away our tent. Several times we woke and gripped the canvas, fearing it would be torn from the guys, and several times the sides were strengthened by additional rocks. It was the same storm that doubtless visited the hunting parties at about that time, although from what I learned they did not get as much wind.

On Thursday morning, soon after midnight, there were signs of clearing, and Dunning, on interviewing Jacob, our one-eyed skipper, finally got him to say he would proceed. We were all anxious to be off; we knew the people on the steamer were worrying about us, and we were afraid of missing the schooners.

Itirdlek, a small, poverty-stricken place of perhaps fifty

souls, was reached at eleven o'clock. The Arctic Circle had been crossed that morning, and for the first time we were really within the Arctic Zone. The news we heard was bad— no schooners, and no knowledge of them. That was the gist of our conversation with Trader Jacob Dahl.

The wind had gone down, and the mosquitoes were making life miserable, when we packed up our effects, after a hasty meal, and prepared for a thirty-mile row. We buckled down to our task in earnest, each one in turn taking a hand at the oars.

At six o'clock that night Amerdlok fiord was crossed, and at eight the town of Holsteinborg, our destination, was sighted. We were greeted with open arms by Governor Müller, who informed us that some five schooners were off the coast only a few miles, one having gone out only that morning.

The effect upon us of this news, the feeling of joy and relief, can be better imagined than described, and when we were ushered into a room where actually there was a bed with eider-down pillows, mattresses, and quilts we for the moment forgot that we were shipwrecked people, and lived entirely in the present.

There was but one hitch in this streak of good luck: we couldn't all sleep in that bed; so we drew lots, and Ladd, Thompson, and I bunked out on the floor. Dr. Cook and Rogers slept on the feathers. Next night, however, I very conveniently became ill, which obviously gave me the right to the bed, so I experienced the pleasant change from rocks and boards to eider-down and linen.

When I awoke next morning I heard these words uttered by Dr. Cook: "Thompson, I want you, Rogers, and Porter to take a telescope and climb that mountain across the harbor to look for a schooner; if you see a sail, note its bearing and return at once." We had no sooner crossed the harbor and begun the ascent than Rogers saw a vessel putting in south of us—at Nepisat, we thought—and he started back immediately to inform the Doctor, while Thompson and I went on up the mountain.

I shall never forget that ascent. First we got into the fog, later into rain, and finally, when about two-thirds of the way up, we found ourselves in a blinding snow-storm. We kept on, and finally reached the summit, some 2,000 feet above the sea-level, glorying in the fact that it was August and that we were knee-deep in snow.

I took several snap shots on this little trip, one in particular of a beautiful waterfall near the base of the mountain, which I regret exceedingly was lost.

I saw my first and only game in Greenland as we were approaching the foot of the mountain in the boat. It was a blue fox, and a small one at that. The little fellow watched us from the shore until we had almost landed, when, with a bark very much like that of a dog, he scampered off over the rocks.

As soon as Dr. Cook heard of the sail we had seen he despatched a kayaker with instructions to intercept the vessel and deliver despatches stating our distress and asking for assistance. For the rest of the day we wandered about the town, taking pictures, and watching the governor exercise his dogs attached to a sledge, which they drew over the lawn in the yard in fine style. At meal times Mr. Muller spread a bountiful repast, at which he insisted we should all be present, and which it is unnecessary to say we all enjoyed immensely after the scanty meals we had coming up the coast.

I cannot speak too highly of this gentleman's courtesy and unbounded hospitality to us while we were under his roof. There was nothing too good for us, and when the time for parting came, sincere regret was expressed by the entire family. They lived in the same comfortable, almost luxurious style as Governor Bistrup, at Sukkertoppen, with all modern conveniences, from a beautiful upright piano down to a snapshot camera.

To return to the mission nearest our hearts. The climax came the second evening, August 16, while we were in the governor's study. There was a commotion at the wharf, and some urchin ran in sputtering something about strangers at the dock, and we all rushed to the gate at the brow of the hill to see what the matter was. Coming up the narrow path was a sight which moved me, and I believe the rest of our little band, more than any other event of the trip, not even excepting the accident.

Swinging from side to side, and clad in their oilskins and sou'westers, were five Gloucester fishermen. They had heard of our mishap, and had come post-haste to Holsteinborg in a dory. The spokesman, a man whose name is now a household word in many homes, was taken into the governor's house and our case was laid before him, and very soon we saw how matters stood. The noble fellow was standing between sympathy and duty. In justice to his crew and the owners of his vessel, he could not abandon his cruise for the sake of a party of unfortunate strangers. Yet such was his love for humanity, seeing that we were staring the prospects of a winter in Greenland in the face, he felt what he would want another man to do if he were in our place. He left us with these words: "I must see my crew. If you see my vessel in the offing to-morrow morning flying her flag you will understand that I have decided to take you to your friends at Sukkertoppen."

The morning came, and with it the schooner. All that which follows is an old story; that is, after we reached our party on August 20. We rowed to the schooner, our effects were put aboard, and our crew of faithful, dirty Huskies left us with the whale-boat to make their way to Sukkertoppen by themselves. The good schooner *Rigel* weathered out a moderate gale off Kangarmuit and finally drew up alongside the *Miranda*, surrounded by the whole of the populace in their boats.

Thus ended ten days of the most delightful experiences of my life. Nothing have I ever given up with a more lingering regret than the sight of "Greenland's icy mountains" fading away in the dim, purple distance.

THE TRIP TO HOLSTEINBORG.

BY MAYNARD LADD.

Mr. Porter has had the pleasant task of telling the story of the trip to Holsteinborg in search of a vessel to bring the passengers and crew of the *Miranda* back to home and friends. I do not wish to encroach upon his ground, and, as I have not seen his narrative, I may prove a trespasser. If this be the case I offer my apologies to Mr. Porter and to whomever may chance to read these fragmentary reminiscences.

We six—Dr. Cook, Porter, Rogers, Thompson, Dunning, and I—enjoyed a novelty of incidents in that eventful trip of ten days which made it to us the most memorable experience of the expedition. My mind dwells with most interest on the first and last days of the journey. Up to the time we stepped down the gangway ladder into the boat and pulled out of the harbor of Sukkertoppen amid the cheers and eager God-speeds of our companions, events had turned from bad to worse, until the good-natured acquiescence of the passengers to their continual ill-luck was surely changing to a feeling of anxious apprehension. In retrospect, it seems as if the spell of misfortune which had followed us with such persistency became broken from the moment we lost sight of the *Miranda* as we rounded the rocky promontory which enclosed the northern part of the harbor.

A favoring breeze freshened our hopes as it speeded us in the direction of Kangarmuit. That evening's sail was rare sport. The wind grew stronger and stronger, driving us along at a pace that left our swift kayaker far astern, and we were finally obliged to lay to under the lee of an island to await his coming. When we had taken him and his canoe aboard we numbered eleven persons, who, with the tents, provisions, and sundry luggage, weighted our twenty-foot boat about to her limit. How well I remember that evening! We six were snugly packed in the stern, our knees locked, and every inch of room occupied. In the bow were the four Huskie sailors, and behind us sat old Jacob Neilson, our half-breed pilot, blind in one eye, but, as we had many opportunities to prove, still skilful in the art of sailing between dangerous shoals and ugly-looking reefs.

Toward eleven o'clock it grew moderately dark, and heavy gusts of wind began to sweep over the water at frequent intervals, gradually increasing in strength. One of the sails had to be taken in, and often the second also, when a particularly heavy blast made the little boat tip to one side until the water flowed over the gunwale. The Huskies, crouched low on the windward side, kept a close lookout for the squalls. Every minute or two came their warning shouts to Jacob, and a moment later the strain upon the masts bore witness to the keen sight of the natives. Our pilot's skill never failed him, however, and we soon acquired confidence in him and the staunch little boat. The shoals and reefs which surrounded us looked ominous in the dusky light, but only once did they seriously threaten us; and then our rudder became unshipped and we were being driven rapidly toward the rocky shore. The oars were quickly put in place, and a little vigorous pulling prevented any accident.

As we neared Kangarmuit we got under the lee of the islands. The sailing grew quiet and less exciting. The

Eskimos relaxed their vigilance, and, crowding close to each other for warmth, sang weird native songs. Cold and fatigued from our cramped position, we dozed as best we could. Morning was dawning as we entered the harbor of Kangarmuit, or Old Sukkertoppen, amid a grand chorus of howls from a colony of dogs, which gave to the slumbering village the first intimation of the presence of strangers.

For several days the wind blew strongly from the southwest and the sea and sky were threatening. If the condition of the elements was at times unfavorable to our plans, it had the redeeming feature of adding to the picturesqueness and impressiveness of the scenery along the coast. We were once encamped on a little island, named by us "Windy Cove," for thirty-six hours, during which the gale, which had been steadily gaining in violence since our first night, finally ended. Not until midnight of the fourth day was the water smooth enough for a boat like ours to venture out. So we made a midnight breakfast, broke up our camp, and at two o'clock in the morning embarked for a run of twenty-two hours to Holsteinborg.

The air was cold and piercing after the storm. If we suffered some discomforts in consequence, we were richly compensated for it by the magnificence of the scenery. The heavy black clouds remained, though the wind had moderated, giving a wild and unnatural look to the rugged coast. North and south, as far as the eye could reach, lay a grand chain of mountain ranges. In distant spots one could see the great white masses of the inland ice, which cast its glare into the sky with intense brightness. Between them and the sea, still spotted with foamy whitecaps, rose a great barrier of mountains split into a hundred ragged peaks. Some projected into the heavens for several thousand feet; some seemed like ruined castles built on impregnable heights, and many ended at the very water's edge in steep precipices that

extended almost perpendicularly from the base to the top.
Between them, the overhanging glaciers dipped into the massive fissures, and deep, beautiful fiords ran for miles back toward the interior. The new-fallen snow completely covered the upper portion of the peaks, its brightness intensified by the dark blue of the mountains below the sharply marked snow-line. As the morning advanced, the sun began to pierce the heavy clouds, making a thousand different lights and shadows, and giving an effect the beauty and grandeur of which were truly inspiring.

Many times we wished the rest of the party might have witnessed these scenes. We began to realize what might have been our enthusiasm for Greenland and Arctic voyages if fate had not so suddenly brought the expedition to an end. I feel that we were most fortunate to have had the opportunity of viewing so much of the Greenland coast. We also had a chance to compare the natives of the different settlements. Kangarmuit did not differ much in character from Sukkertoppen, except that it was smaller and the Eskimos were, on the whole, less prosperous. In Itirdlek, however, one could not fail to notice the contrast. The natives were abjectly poor and dirty, and their houses, as a rule, were far worse than those of the most degraded in Sukkertoppen.

In Holsteinborg all was different. An air of comparative respectability and prosperity impressed itself upon us at once. A suspicion of cleanliness, both of the houses and inhabitants, was very evident, and after our visits at Kangarmuit and Itirdlek we felt we had reached Greenland's metropolis. The neat and spacious quarters of Governor Müller and his assistant, Herr Koch, and the government buildings for the seal-oil industry, naturally formed the bulk of the settlement. Perhaps our royal reception at the hands of Governor Müller and his hospitable wife had much to do with our favorable impressions of the place. They certainly showed us every kindness and courtesy. If it had not been for the active services of the Governor in our behalf, the result of our trip would probably have been very different.

As the anniversary of the events related in this history of the *Miranda's* last voyage recurs we all undoubtedly find our thoughts reverting to the scenes through which we passed. I venture to say that in these contributions from the different members of the expedition there will be at least one point of agreement—we are all glad we went, and doubly glad to have happened upon so noble a rescuer as Captain Dixon, of the *Rigel*.

ICEBERGS.

BY ARTHUR R. THOMPSON.

FROM the far Northland ceaselessly
  they come,
Like errant knights, a-sailing
  down the sea,
That alien men may guess the
  majesty
And splendor of the mighty Frost
  King's home.

Firm and immutable they seem,
  and fling
The baffled surges back in high
  disdain,
As if such puny onsets must be vain
'Gainst the proud structures of the Arctic King.

Well might old minstrels sing the monarch's fame
  Within those steel-blue caverns of the ice,
  Where crystal arches, carved in fretwork nice,
His lavish wealth and royal power proclaim.

But as I listen, 'tis no song I hear;
  No hoary minstrel from his cavern sings,
  Nor with enfeebled fingers tunes the strings:
A sound more stern, more awful, meets my ear.

Hark! from the depths of yonder glistening mass
   Come thunderings, as if the mighty Thor
   Had made his fortress there, and offered war
To Ocean's monsters from a throne of glass.

Yet sea-birds shy, as 'twere no fearsome place,
   Alight and rest, and dolphins round it play
   Within the circle of its surf and spray:
Men only turn in terror from its face.

So trend the monsters southward haughtily,
   Admired, and feared, and wondrous for a time,
   Till 'neath the soft, insidious southern clime
They fall—the prey of Sun and fawning Sea.

A GREENLAND SUNDAY.

BY CHARLES BLAKE CARPENTER.

IT WAS a curious but reverently conducted service that we attended at St. James' Church, Sukkertoppen, on August 12. It was a cold, gray misty morning; such a one as in the land of Christian civilization would have soothingly induced the indifferent church-goer to remain quietly at home, conscientiously absorbed in the quantity of his Sunday journal. But the Eskimos —let this virtue be duly regarded— are not fair-weather Christians, and the congregation was large, in consequence. The ladies have no gowns to ruin, no feathers to uncurl, no frizzes to "come out;" nor do silk hats or creased trousers concern the gentlemen. In a pouring rain, therefore, with no umbrellas, all maintain a cheerful countenance and a peace of mind not even remotely disturbed by a shadow of "things correct" as to cut or shape—and go to church. In singular contrast is this spirit to the immortal utterance of one of New England's daughters who, in a contemplative mood, remarks: "There is a repose in the consciousness of being perfectly well dressed that even religion cannot bestow." The revelation of this truth has yet to dawn upon the Eskimo mind. When it does, together with other truths of a highly enlightened nature, the repose in primitive simplicity on the part of the

Greenlanders—that happy independence of a contented people—will be forfeited.

It was the novelty of the situation that induced the American contingent of that singularly strange congregation to be present at a service than which nothing but the spirit in which it was held could be appreciated.

At ten o'clock we were all at the church—a whitewashed stone building with a wooden front, the wood having been brought from Denmark—whose spire, surmounted by a cross, manifests in a strong and beautiful way how in every tribe and kindred the symbol of Christianity is being uplifted. It was not long ago that these people were pagans, and farther north and on the eastern coast many still hold to the crude belief of their forefathers. In the spring of 1894 the first missionary station on the eastern shores was established. The work and zeal of missions are spreading, though marked results are hard to determine. The first bell had called together a motley number, who stood idly about the doors of the church, smiling good-naturedly, and maintaining a respectful silence. At the ringing of the second bell more church-comers hurried from their little igloos. No one entered until Mr. Petersen first went in. Mr. Petersen, a half-breed, studied at Copenhagen for two years, and is the licensed catechist of the parish, as well as the village schoolmaster. His father, an old man with a kind face, assists him. The service is Lutheran. Once each year a regular priest visits the parish to confirm, administer the sacraments, and perform the marriage rites. Marriage is the outcome of an exceedingly brief courtship, during which there is no time allowed for "Huyler's" or flowers to be sentimentally bestowed; in fact, there is nothing pathetically civilized about an Eskimo engagement, but, through Christian influence, let it be said, marriage is honorably regarded.

At the service on this morning in question Mr. Petersen,

Sr., officiated, and his son presided at the organ. The front pews had been reserved for us, and in our rear this strange congregation—the men on one side and the women on the other—arranged themselves, the children sitting in front of them, upon whom the watchful eye could rest and interrupt any enthusiastic diversions from the service itself. A period of the most violent coughing ensued, consumption being common among them—a result of careless living and the mixture of the Danish and Eskimo races.

The interior of the church was neatly painted in white and light-blue, the altar covered with a cloth of red, with *fleur de lis* embroidered in gold. On the altar were two eucharistic lights and a crucifix. Completing the chancel's furnishings were the lectern and old-fashioned pulpit, and a small reed organ. A stove in which peat is burned, near the centre of the nave, afforded the necessary heat. The service was begun in a low, tearful voice, and maintained throughout in the same monotone. While nothing, of course, could be understood by us, the service was nevertheless impressive. A few opening sentences were first read, then the Lord's Prayer; a chant followed, sung in perfect harmony, but very slowly. The Eskimos have good voices and an excellent sense of harmony. It took fifteen minutes to sing this chant. A chapter was then read, after which, for the first time, the congregation rose to repeat some short versicle. A very unimpassioned sermon of twenty-three minutes was read, during which one man gave way to occasional snores. At the close of the sermon they arose for the ascription. A hymn followed, then a prayer and the grace, and the service was ended. At six o'clock that evening we returned for our own service. To my surprise, there were about two hundred Eskimos waiting around the church. It was a most curious congregation, and impressed me singularly. In the front pews sat some of our university professors, several physicians, lawyers, men of business, college students, the Danish Governor, his wife and family, the Assistant Governor and his wife, about thirty of the *Miranda's* crew, and in the rear, closely seated together, were the Huskies, the peculiar fashion of wearing the hair, with their various-colored ribbons, producing a strange effect. A sermon of Dr. Liddon's was read. An Eskimo organist played the hymns which I had arranged, through Mrs. Bistrup, the governor's wife, as interpreter, should be played in the order as marked when I shook my head. We sang "Blest Be the Tie That Binds," "Abide with Me," "Nearer, My God, to Thee," and "Coronation."

> "Let every kindred, every tribe,
> On this terrestrial ball,
> To Him all majesty ascribe,
> And crown Him Lord of all."

seemed fittingly appropriate. "From Greenland's Icy Mountains" would have been gladly sung, but our chances of remaining there for one whole year seemed unpleasantly certain.

The church was provided with no alms-basin, and when the offertory sentence was announced Commodore Gardner passed Mr. Cleveland's hat among our own members of the congregation, and the offering was afterwards presented to the governor, to be used for the benefit of the church. Fortunately, the organist played the hymns in the order of their announcement, and the service proceeded reverently. Though it is a sad reflection, it cannot be denied that Professor Dyche was prominently asleep—a lethargic effect, in all probability, of the Greenland mountain air.

I could not but be impressed, as we read that evening in the Psalter for the twelfth day, with the force of the words: "Thou that art the hope of all the ends of the earth and of them that remain in the broad sea;" and again, "They that dwell in the uttermost parts of the earth shall be afraid at Thy tokens." And then it seemed sad to think how utterly lost must be the meaning of those words that follow in the same beautiful Psalm: "Thou waterest her furrows, Thou sendest rain into the little valleys thereof, Thou makest it soft with the drops of rain and blessest the increase of it. Thou crownest the year with Thy goodness, and Thy clouds drop fatness. They shall drop upon the dwellings of the wilderness, and the little hills shall rejoice on every side. The folds shall be full of sheep, the valleys also shall stand so thick with corn that they shall laugh and sing." Eskimos have no idea of furrows. They have never seen sheep, nor sheep-folds, nor corn. The beauty is lost to them, and they are not aware of the existence of so many of our most familiar things. Fortunately, in no way is this knowledge necessary for their practical welfare or happiness. The hard, cold facts of Arctic theology must be referred to some native doctor of divinity for consistent explanation. Emerging in comparatively recent times from the strange superstitions of which their folk-lore tells us, their appreciation of some of the fundamental doctrines of the Christian religion has yet to develop. Christian influence, however, has brought about many changes, and they are wisely instructed in religion in a natural native way, without the unnecessary accompaniments of a foreign civilization being thrust upon them—their means of living not admitting of these advantages. Far better for them to know and feel the real truth of religion according to their own standard of civilization, however crude that may seem—to be taught their duty in that state of life in which God has placed them—than to introduce a civilization which would breed a spirit of discontent and lead to the extermination of the race.

After church we were delightfully entertained by the governor and his family, and so our Sunday amid Greenland's icy mountains came to an end, leaving impressions which will long be pleasantly remembered.

OUR ADVENTURES AT SUKKERTOPPEN

BY CARLYLE GARRISON.

AT GOVERNOR BISTRUP'S house we were heartily welcomed. On August 9 we started for Disco. A storm seemed impending, and the wind was blowing half a gale. Captain Farrell's charts were old, so he had to rely on the pilot who took us out.

The pilot left us about 8 A. M., after giving directions to Captain Farrell. What these were, opinions differ. However, when we had steamed about seven miles on our course, and were still near the rocky shores, our ship met with the accident that eventually caused us to abandon her.

About half-past eight o'clock, while we were all at breakfast, a slight grating was heard, then it ceased for a moment; but as the *Miranda* sank into the trough of the sea she crashed down upon a hidden reef, throwing men from their feet and piling the dishes indiscriminately at one end of the dining-room—and the third time that she came down on the reef we all felt instinctively that the ship would sink, so a scramble for the deck occurred, thus rendering the companionway a scene of the wildest excitement.

But when we arrived on deck the confusion was over, and those who were sparsely attired even ventured to go below and finish their toilet. To show how the mind acts under intense excitement, one man rushed to his stateroom and gravely told his companion to save all the tobacco that he had. The latter carefully poured from a tin box about three pipe-loads of the sacred stuff and tied it up in a paper bag; then remembering the ship's condition, he rushed on deck.

The whistle was blown and the cannon fired so as to attract the attention of those on shore.

After waiting some time we saw two small specks appear on the crest of a wave, but in another instant they had disappeared. Now the specks would appear and disappear at short intervals, and again we would lose sight of them for some time. Finally they reached the side of the *Miranda*, and proved to be kayaks. Climbing up the ladder, the first Eskimo, rushing to the bridge where the captain stood, pointed over the starboard bow, and exclaimed, in an excited tone, "No goot!" then pointing to his mouth, he wavered as though he were about to fall. The battle with the waves had completely exhausted him. Water was soon brought to him, and had the desired effect.

About an hour later we were moored in the harbor of Sukkertoppen. The engineer made an examination, and found that the water-ballast tank was filled with water and could not be cleared. He also found two small holes, which were immediately plugged. In such a condition it was impossible to attempt to cross Davis Straits, so we must hunt for aid.

We learned that several American fishing schooners were anchored at Holsteinborg, about one hundred and forty miles north of Sukkertoppen. The outlook was not very pleasant, for if we did not get another ship we should have to winter in Greenland, which meant probable death to some of us.

Dr. Cook got up a party to go to Holsteinborg. He procured a boat from Governor Bistrup. It was twenty-four feet long, carrying two sails, with five Eskimos to manage it. Two other parties went out for pleasure: one under Professor Wright, of Oberlin College, to visit the glaciers, and the other under Henry Collins Walsh, the historian of the party, to kill reindeer.

During the two weeks that we remained in Greenland we had many opportunities of seeing the characteristics of the Eskimos. At a dance given in the governor's yard a young man from the *Miranda* failed to find a partner, but soon an Eskimo, seeing him looking on, brought his wife to dance with him. After the dance the Eskimo came up to him and said, "Un crowner," meaning that he wanted a crown for letting his wife dance, but I am afraid that he failed to collect the money.

THE ILLUSTRATIONS.

BY RUDOLF KERSTING,
OFFICIAL PHOTOGRAPHER.

SEVENTEEN cameras on board the *Miranda*, and seventeen minds differing in their objects and views. Had the steamer been able to go over the intended route and given the travellers the time proposed, never would a more complete pictorial record of Arctic travel, sport, and scientific aspects have been made. As it was, the scope of subjects in the illustrations is much more varied than any one, two, or three men, amateur or professional, could have procured.

Something over a thousand plates, mostly developed, were lost when the steamer was abandoned. The writer lost over six hundred eight by ten negatives.

The illustrations in this book are products of the cameras of members of the expedition, with the exception of five. These were reproduced from originals taken by a native Eskimo photographer at Godthaab, who spent two years in Denmark, and is quite proficient in the art; and two of the illustrations have been reproduced from sketches. A few remarks concerning the photographers and their work will add to the interest of the illustrations.

Professor William H. Brewer, of Yale, photographed with excellent success, paying much attention to lighting his sub-

 W. H. BREWER
 G. FRED'K WRIGHT
 F. B. WRIGHT
 JAMES D. DEWELL

 C. B. CARPENTER
 RUD. KERSTING
 E. P. LYON

 R. O. STEBBINS
 R. W. PORTER
 A. P. ROGERS
 J. R. FORDYCE

 G. W. GARDNER
 JULES F. VALLÉ
 L. L. DYCHE
 A. R. THOMPSON
 A. B. BROWN

jects, the geological formations of rocks, dikes, traps, and eruptive basalt.

Professor G. Fred. Wright, of Oberlin, and his son Fred, an able assistant, were especially interested in glacial formations, photographing glacier fronts, tops, moraines, etc. Their views are among the best, as far as execution and selection of subjects are concerned. Unfortunately, many of their finest views were lost.

James D. Dewell, using a camera for the first time, astonished every one with the fine results of his work. He was interested particularly in the subject of cemeteries, and to this we are indebted for the fine views of Sukkertoppen Cemetery and its beautiful scenic surroundings. Charles B. Carpenter, a theological student, also handling a camera for the first time, had the good fortune to save all of his photographs —about one hundred and seventy in number. The majority of illustrations in this book are from his work. Thanks to his turn of mind, we have, among others, pictures of the church, the Petersen family, and the governors and their families.

Elias P. Lyon, professor of biology, naturally contributed scenes and views particularly appropriate to his studies.

Roswell O. Stebbins, D.D.S., had the misfortune to lose about three hundred negatives, the majority relating to his study of the formation of Eskimo teeth and jaws. Thanks to his magazine camera, we have a dozen views of the expedition up Isortok fiord, of which he was a member. Photographs by him, taken on the return trip after reaching Labrador, are unquestionably the best extant.

Russell W. Porter also lost all his Greenland views, but contributes a few good illustrations from life on board the *Rigel*. A. P. Rogers saved two plates, which are the only pictures we have of First Mate Manuel and Ice-pilot Dumphy. John R. Fordyce also saved his entire collection, numbering about two hundred.

All the above-mentioned gentlemen saved more or less of their work, but the following lost their negatives and cameras: Dr. Jules F. Vallé, for twenty years a noted amateur, had undoubtedly the finest collection of native character-studies ever collected. Professor L. L. Dyche, the naturalist, Commodore G. W. Gardner, A. R. Thompson, and A. B. Brown trusted too much to the staunchness of the *Miranda*, and have nothing for their labor.

Never did a set of men work more harmoniously, earnestly, and enthusiastically than did my friends, the amateur photographers of the Cook Arctic Expedition of 1894.

A LETTER FROM HON. GEO. W. GARDNER.

DEAR OLD SHIPMATE:—From the moil and turmoil of a business life, I rest to think over the haps and mishaps occurring to that royal good company who trusted themselves to an ill-fitted and ill-fated iron steamship which sailed her final cruise, ending disastrously and yet so fortunately for us, though she now lies in the depths of the great northern sea. Shall we ever forget her name—the *Miranda*—or the ceaseless, untiring efforts for a successful voyage on the part of her good commander, or the noble-hearted captain who, with his whole-souled crew, rescued us by giving up an opportunity for financial success, in deviating from the object of his trip, generously providing us, in his good ship the *Rigel*, a safe passage to an accessible port, that we might continue on in the light of this life and its enjoyments with those most dear to us? So long as this life lasts, we certainly shall not.

What a transition, from the horrors of a shipwrecked condition—the insatiable longing for something palatable when afar off on Greenland's icy shore, patiently, hopefully waiting for succor—to the courteous hospitality of good Governor Bistrup, who never before spoke an English word till, with our teaching, he uttered that well-known sentence, "Many happy days," and to Mrs. Governor Bistrup, his charming wife, who in a most kindly manner greeted us so warmly that the chill of the Arctic air was dissipated, and we moved in the thirty-third degree of Danish Greenland social enjoyment. What a change from the time when we were studying latitude and longitude, dodging the treacherous ice-fields that persistently surrounded us, peering in dense fogs that ever followed us, and fearing the almost certainty of dangerous reefs beneath us. You haven't forgotten, dear old shipmate—for our companionship 'midst all the discomforts of a dangerous cruise made us dear, each to the other—you cannot have forgotten the delicious enjoyment of that, to us, odd but elegant dinner given us by our friends, Governor and Mrs. Bistrup, in their dove-nest, the only civilized—though small in compass—residence in that community of happy, peaceable, dirty Eskimos, who informed us in the good Huskie language that we all learned to know that Sukkertoppen was the name of the settlement where, with *them*, seal meat as fat as the Huskies who ate it raw was the staple diet. But we were not obliged eat it, for our governor's family were endowed with the greatest of social virtues, a generous hospitality, the more appreciated because the less anticipated.

How we wondered whence came those dishes, served so graciously and with such congeniality, without ostentatious display, and how good they tasted to the starving explorers! Deer sausage, prepared like Hamburg steaks, a fish dish tasting not unlike and resembling head-cheese, green peas, fruit, jam, radishes—real fresh radishes—about the size of a hazel nut, grown during the only month of Greenland sunny weather in the governor's garden of actual soil—a garden about ten feet by four—a wonderful garden of this one vegetable, for be it known that Greenland's strands are but rock, snow, and ice. Excuse this digression, but I felt obliged to explain how it came that we had fresh radishes. To these were added black and white bread, Danish butter, pickles, schnapps, sherry, madeira, and beer. Then followed the dessert of wafers, Swiss cheese, bread, coffee with goat's milk, brandy, and cigars.

No epicure could have been more agreeably surprised with a "feast fit for the gods" than was this Arctic shipwrecked party with the dainties so freely given by our generous hosts.

And now, good friend, comes the query: what benefit to man have these Arctic explorations wrought? A knowledge of the natives of the wild northern wastes, whose origin is unknown, their habits and mode of living, of the formation of glaciers and their movements, the presence of whales, cod, halibut, and of innumerable marine birds and polar bears, and a cryolite formation, is about the sum and substance; yet so long as the faith of nations, of historical and scientific associations, and of purse-plethoric individuals is not exhausted, the ambitious will continue attempts that are always fraught with privations, horrible suffering, and death to fathom the mysterious, if not mythical, elusive North Pole; to render possible the determination of the lines of variation in the magnetic needle, for which mariners would be eternally grateful, and to discover a northwest passage that would never be frequented. Is it worth the while? Old shipmate, let you and me give all the chance and glory for future, probably futile, attempts to those who think they like heroic martyrdom.

GEORGE W. GARDNER.

To H. C. WALSH.

A LETTER FROM PROF. B. C. JILLSON.

MY DEAR MR. WALSH:—You ask me to write something for your Arctic book concerning that part of our trip which most interested me. Now, my dear fellow, should I comply with your request, you would receive a volume as big as Webster's Dictionary, for every moment of the two months and a half was full of intense interest— some of it too intense to be particularly pleasant.

The icebergs made an impression on me not easily effaced. How large they were, and how beautiful! Huge cubical blocks of ice measuring hundreds of feet on a side, reflecting the light like a mirror, or sparkling like ten thousand diamonds; large "hay stacks," as white as the driven snow, floating on a polished sea; grand old cathedrals, with their turrets and towers and pinnacles and steeples; enormous fortifications with perpendicular sides, their tops crowned with battlements, with embrasures for cannon and long cracks like loop-holes for musketry. And what beautiful plays of colors were produced as the light was reflected from their sides and from the deep crevices, or from the caves and caverns studded with icicles, making the mass glow with green and blue, like a huge topaz, or emerald, or amethyst! and these beautiful sights we witnessed day after day, never the same, but always varying in form and color.

Do you remember that night when we were lost off the coast of Labrador and rowed from 6 A. M. till 2:30 P. M.

before we reached the ship? Oh, how cold it was! and when we landed on that island how I shivered, and how the others —good fellows as they were—almost smothered me with blankets and overcoats; and how my chattering teeth bit off the stem of a pipe before I had taken a single puff; and how we ran and danced, and swung our arms to keep the blood in motion! And that same night how the auroras streaked the sky, now here, now there, with their long lines of quivering light looking like spears in the trembling hands of giants! And afterwards on the *Rigel*, what a magnificent aurora that was swinging over our heads, its great folds beaming with rose and purple light, trembling as though shaken by some mysterious power! And another night on the *Miranda*, when a rainbow appeared longer and wider than any we had ever seen, with the most beautiful and varying tints, with streamers shooting upward and downward from the great arch, and with the trembling, wavy motion so characteristic of the "Merry Dancers of the North."

I remember you were in the party that took two dories and rowed twenty-four miles up the Isortok fiord, in Greenland, to visit some glaciers. What a fine sight was that we witnessed on our return, as the sun sank behind that long line of mountains whose top, notched like a saw, was clear cut against the sky. What exquisite colors: how they changed and varied in tint, and how long the twilight lasted, with its after-glow! Mr. Stokes, the artist of Peary's first expedition, gave an exhibition here in Pittsburgh of his paintings of Arctic scenery, sunsets, auroras, etc. Nearly every one who saw these views thought them exaggerated—that such a coloring of nature was impossible. We know better, for we have seen it, not once or twice, but repeated and varied day after day and night after night; to see such colors is worth all it costs, even if one loses all his worldly goods and is obliged to come home on a fishing smack.

When the *Miranda* lay in the harbor of Sukkertoppen, a few hours after your party had started on a hunting trip, myself and seven others, with five Eskimos, left to study the glaciers at the head of Ikamiut fiord. For eleven days we lived in a small tent pitched on a narrow neck of land where two fiords meet. It was cold and stormy, and we were subjected to many inconveniences, but were amply repaid by the result of our studies and by living in the midst of such grand scenery, with such strange surroundings. We had for neighbors fifteen natives—nine women and six men—who lived in two igloos—miserable huts made of rough stone covered with sod. We were surrounded by solid rocks, which rose straight from the water a thousand or more feet, their tops covered with snow and ice which extended in long arms nearly to the water's edge. Several glaciers were in view, and our ears were frequently saluted by the boom! boom! like the discharge of heavy artillery, as icebergs broke from the parent mass and floated away. As we rowed over the fiords, or climbed the rough rocks, or wandered over the glaciers, not a tree was to be seen—not a shrub. Only a little grass between the rocks and a few flowers gave life to this "Land of Desolation."

On Sunday we held service, to which our Eskimo friends were invited. The front of our tent was thrown back, and we sat at the entrance, while before us on our boat-seats were the natives clothed in their picturesque costumes made of fur. Of course, we did not omit that grand old missionary hymn, "From Greenland's Icy Mountains," and we sang it, too, as we never sang it before, for were we not in the midst of those very mountains covered with ice and snow, and those wonderful fiords with their floating icebergs? Is it any wonder that our thoughts frequently wandered to that far distant land where our friends were worshipping with such different surroundings?

Why, my dear fellow, everything interested me. Every day brought something new and strange. I believe I could write volumes about the magnificent scenery of Greenland and its wonderful system of glaciers and fiords ; about the funny little women with divided skirts, their heads adorned with red and blue and green ribbons and crowned with a Psyche knot, while perhaps a little bright-eyed baby cooed from the golf hood on the back of its mother ; about the kayakers and their remarkable kayaks, how they would glide over the stormy sea where no white man dared venture, and how they would roll over and over, now in the water and now out, wetting only their hands and face. And their harpoons! how ingeniously they were made, as well as their weapons for capturing the seal, walrus, and other game—but why write more ? Every day was full of interest, from the rising of the sun to the going down thereof. Only yesterday a man said to me, " I never heard of any one who went in the vicinity of the North Pole who didn't want to go again, and you are another of those Arctic cranks. I don't understand it." Well, we do ; we've been there.

I cannot close without a word of praise for good Captain Dixon and his crew, who came to our rescue when in dire distress, and, with great pecuniary loss and inconvenience, took us to a place of safety. They are a good type of the New England fishermen—brave, venturesome, kind-hearted, and ever ready to help the unfortunate. May God bless each one of them with a long and happy life.

B. C. Jillson.

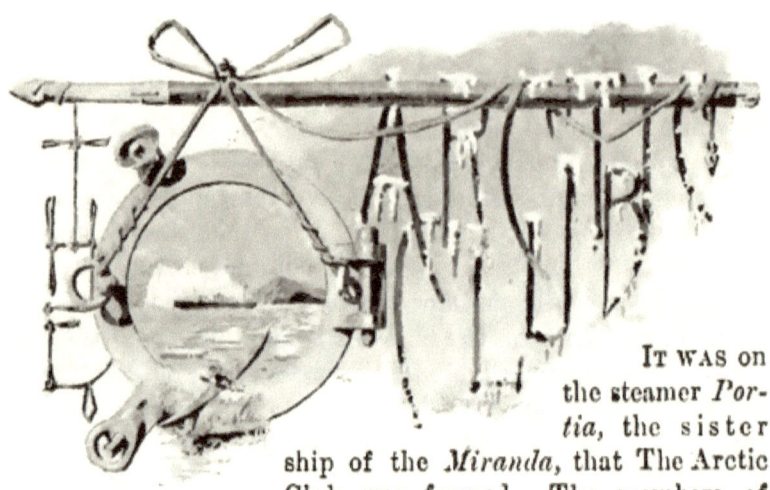

IT WAS on the steamer *Portia*, the sister ship of the *Miranda*, that The Arctic Club was formed. The members of Dr. Cook's Arctic Expedition of 1894, homeward bound on that vessel, met in the smoking-room on the evening of September 8 and organized a club whose active members should consist of all the persons upon the passenger list of the *Miranda* on her last cruise into Arctic waters. The following officers were elected: Professor William H. Brewer, president; Mr. Henry Collins Walsh, secretary; and Mr. Rudolf Kersting, treasurer. Motions were passed to this effect: That an annual dinner be given by the club at a date falling between Christmas and New Year's Day; and that any members unable to attend should forward letters to the secretary to be read at the dinner.

The following gentlemen were elected honorary members of the club: Captain George W. Dixon, of Gloucester, Mass.; Captain William J. Farrell, of New York; Governor Bistrup and Assistant-Governor Baumann, of Sukkertoppen, and Governor Müller, of Holsteinborg, Greenland. The members of the expedition had already been bound together by the strong ties of common experiences, hardships, and dangers. It seemed well, therefore, to appoint a certain time when these experiences could be retold over the walnuts and wine. After Æneas and his weary Trojans had been toiling against wind and wave he cheered their drooping spirits by remarking to them, "*Forsan et haec olim meminisse juvabit.*" And in truth there is nothing pleasanter in life in the way of social entertainment than the recalling of common hardships and dangers about a board where old comrades have assembled, and where libations and the incense of cigars are offered to the rescuing gods.

The first annual dinner of the Arctic Club took place at the Hotel Martin, New York, on December 27, 1894, and was a unique and enjoyable affair. Speeches descriptive of Arctic life and adventure were made, and incidents and recollections of the trip were recalled by Professor William H. Brewer, Mr. James D. Dewell, Hon. George W. Gardner, Captain William J. Farrell, Dr. R. M. Cramer, Chief Officer George Manuel, Dr. R. O. Stebbins, Professor L. J. W. Joyner, Dr. Frederick A. Cook, Mr. A. P. Rogers, Mr. Rudolf Kersting, Mr. Frederick P. Gay, Mr. William J. Littell, Mr. H. D. Cleveland, Mr. George M. Coates, Jr., and Mr. Carlyle Garrison.

Letters of regret were read from various members of the club who were unable to attend the dinner; among these was one from Captain George W. Dixon, who, unfortunately, was detained by business in Gloucester. Mr. Henry Collins Walsh gave a toast in his honor. In explanation of a certain portion of this toast, it must be said that the passengers of the *Miranda* had subscribed, before they parted at Sydney, the sum of two hundred and fifty dollars for the purchase of some fitting testimonial to Captain Dixon; a large old-fashioned clock, richly ornamented, being finally decided upon by the committee appointed for the purpose of purchasing the testimonial. This clock, with an appropriate inscription upon a silver plate, was accordingly forwarded to Captain Dixon early in October, 1894.

THE TOAST.

I drink to one, he is not here,
  Yet I would guard his glory ;
A knight without reproach or fear
  Should live in song and story.

No knight is he of high degree,
  Who fought for fame and beauty ;
But just a sailor of the sea
  Who did his seaman's duty

He thought of others, not of self,
  That night our good ships parted ;
Nor cared for salvage nor for pelf,
  Because so human-hearted.

For unto him his fellow-men
  Were the most precious burden ;
And aught else was of lesser ken,
  Nor recked he of his guerdon.

And is he now upon the sea,
  Or with his dear ones round him,
Like carriers, may our greetings be,
  And rest not till they've found him.

One memory like the golden sands
  Down Time's glass ever flowing,
Our tall clock stands, and points its hands
  To his coming and his going.

And when he comes to meat and bread,
  I know 'tis but a fiction,
And yet, methinks the clock hands spread
  To give our benediction.

Till hearts are dead, till eyes are dim,
  We shall forget him never;
And may our blessings bide with him
  Forever and forever.

So I drink to one, he is not here,
  Yet I would guard his glory:
A knight without reproach or fear
  Should live in song and story.

A heart as gentle as a lass,
  Yet bold as any eagle;
O comrades, rise! I fill this glass
  To Dixon of the *Rigel!*